We consider the universe as an open book. The Holy Quran then emerges as an open book of the universe, a clear book of wisdom and science:

> *"These are the Ayat (i.e. verses, lessons, evidence, and proofs) of Allah, which We recite to you with truth. Then, in which speech after Allah and His Ayat will they believe?"*
>
> (Quran 45:6).

As one of His beautiful Names is "The Truth" the search for truth is a foundational requirement of the Holy Quran. Therefore, Allah calls on Muslims to study the universe and recognize the Divine Laws for managing celestial and terrestrial affairs. From this perspective, two Divine Forces and some Divine Laws are presented in this book.

The book includes some aspects of natural sciences found in the Holy Quran and some pioneering scientific accomplishments of the Islamic civilization. When Muslims will give knowledge, ethics, and scientific research their due place, Muslims will return to their prime, and the book makes a strong case for this approach.

Natural Sciences in the Mirror of Islam

Natural Sciences in the Mirror of Islam

Zin Eddine Dadach

MV Publishers

Published by MV Publishers, a subsidiary of Muslim Voice,
12719 Hillmeade Station Dr, Bowie, MD 20720, USA.
MVPublishers@muslimvoice.org

ISBN 978-1-956601-24-4

First edition 2025

United States of America

Zin Eddine Dadach, 1957 –

Muslim Voice

ISBN 978-1-956601-24-4

to my mother

Contents

"Surely your Lord is Allah Who created the heavens and the Earth in six Days, then established Himself on the Throne, conducting every affair."

(Quran 10:3)

To My Dearest Mother

"We have enjoined on man kindness to his parents: In pain did his mother bear him, and in pain did she give him birth… "

(Quran 46:15)

We all carry precious memories of our mothers' love and the sacrifices they made. For me, these memories are painted in the colors of the early seventies. It was the first time I left my family to study in the high school Faradj in the city of Tilimsen, located about 70 km from my hometown, Beni Saf. I used to return to Beni Saf after spending two weeks in the high school dormitory. Upon my arrival home, I always found my mother waiting—warm coffee in one hand, a plate of her homemade cookies in the other. As we sat together, she would listen intently while I shared stories of my new life at school, her eyes reflecting both pride and concern. She always appeared concerned, asking questions like, "Are you eating enough?" "Is it not too cold for you?" "Do you have enough money?" After our discussion, she would take the dirty laundry from my bag.

Leaving our home, I would often spend a long time listening to music on my tiny radio while walking through the cliffside of the city. My dreams were mixed with the fragrance of the pine trees and the quietness of the Mediterranean Sea. Whenever I return home, I always find my mother in the kitchen. It was, in fact, her headquarters, and she was there most of the day. She often prepared our meals and, at other times, washed dishes or cleaned fish. Additionally, she would handwash all the family's clothes and occasionally make jam from seasonal fruits.

After every weekend with my family, Saturday mornings were always the same. My mother would wake me up at 4 a.m. because the bus leaves at 6 a.m. While I quietly sipped my coffee, she used to iron my clothes and put them carefully in my bag. One particular morning stands frozen in my memory. My mother approached me with that gentle smile I knew so well and said, "My son, you are always so quiet. I wonder what secrets your heart keeps from us. When I kissed her to leave for the bus station, she would pack some cookies and give me the extra money.

I had this beautiful relationship with my mother throughout my three years in high school. In September 1975, when I joined an engineering college near Algiers, I could visit my parents only during religious holidays and summer vacations, when Allah called my mother to her eternal rest. These precious memories flooded back, each one a testament to her boundless love. Even now, they move me to tears. Since then, I have prayed to Allah (SWT) that her abode will be in Heaven this time.

Ameen.

Foreword

In the name of Allah, the Most Gracious, the Most Merciful

Praise be to Allah (SWT), Lord of the Worlds, and may blessings and peace be upon our Prophet Muhammad, and those who follow him and are guided by him until the Day of Judgment.

Having studied natural sciences following the Western philosophy and atheism, reading this book was a truly enriching experience. It explores the profound and beautiful relationship between Islam and the sciences of natural phenomena. I felt as if I were discovering new treasures in the Quran and Sunnah, revealing a beautiful harmony between our faith and our pursuit of knowledge. What struck me most was the concept of the "Islamization" of science. The book invites Muslim scholars to draw inspiration from the Holy Quran and Sunnah in our study of the universe. This connection has given a whole new meaning to the natural sciences for Muslim students.

Overall, this book is more than just an informative read; it is a roadmap for exploring the beautiful relationship between our faith and natural sciences. This book is undoubtedly a valuable resource on my journey toward a deeper understanding of Islam and the universe. I believe this book is of immense value to the entire Ummah and humanity. It encourages a deeper understanding of the Holy Quran and strengthens our faith by demonstrating its wonderful harmony with the natural world.

This book serves as a valuable resource for Muslim students and scholars seeking to integrate their faith with knowledge.

Mohammad Ali
Director, CEO
Madrasatut Taqwa Al Islamia (Islamic School)
& Islamic Online Madrasha BD
Bangladesh

Dhu'l-Hijjah 12, 1446 AH corresponding to 8th of June of 2025

Preface

"And whoever fears Allah - He will make for him a way out and will provide for him from where he does not expect. And whoever relies upon Allah - then He is sufficient for him"

(Quran 65:2-3)

When I obtained my bachelor's degree from a technical school in Algeria, I had the opportunity to continue my graduate studies and work in different cities worldwide. These living and educational experiences allowed me to learn about very different aspects of natural sciences by conducting experiments in research laboratories, but also to discover the diverse facets of human nature by interacting with people of different cultures, religions, and social backgrounds.

When I first set foot in New York in October 1980, I entered a world unlike anything I had known. Here, I wasn't just studying science; I was learning the deeper science of human connection across cultures and faiths. I especially had fun picking up some words from various international languages and dialects. Being for the first time in a hotel for international students called "International House", I remember spending my first months trying to guess the country and the language of the students I crossed in the hotel's corridors. After some time, I could remember some names and became friends with some residents.

Arriving in Quebec City (Canada) in January of 1990, I realized that the French language has a very different accent from the one spoken in France, and the interaction of the local people with nature taught me many lessons. For example, I was surprised to see some people very impatiently waiting for the first snowstorm of the long and icy winter. I realized later that winter in Quebec City is not only a season but also part of their cultural heritage. I also remember going to Laval University one day of February of 1992, while a northern wind was blowing, and the sky had a magic blue color. On my way to the bus stop, I met a few people, and they were completely wrapped up in warm clothes. That day the temperature reached $- 50° C$ with the wind-chill factor, and I felt my face burning. As I was walking very fast to avoid freezing, I thought that hell is not only about fire but could also be about extremely cold temperatures. I also learned during this long, cold winter that patience is the best cure for hardship.

When I landed in Osaka (Japan) in November of 1994, I felt like I was on a different planet. Every bit of wisdom I learned in New York City and Quebec City was almost useless. My most challenging experience is that people don't always tell you what they think, but what pleases you. This is called "Harmony" in Japan. For example, to have a welcoming start, a party was organized for me in a restaurant where all the members of the research group seemed very relaxed and happy talking to me. However, when I started my work the next week, I was surprised to notice that nobody seemed to know me anymore. I also learned that Japanese society is a "group society", and parents teach their children how to behave in society, like parents in other countries teach their children about religion.

While living in these cities, I saw some people using cutlery to eat, whereas others used their hands or chopsticks. However, I knew that everyone was eating for sustenance and survival. Similarly, I heard many languages and dialects, but everyone had the same common need to communicate and express human feelings. My best experience as a human being was in New York City when some friends of different cultures found love and embarked on intercultural marriages. Indeed, during a wedding ceremony of a Turkish friend and a Korean lady, I asked myself, "Why is love stronger than the difference in cultures?" One day in the Fall of 1982, I attended a cultural event organized at International House. During the colorful event, I saw international students wearing their different colorful dresses; I also heard many types of international music and tasted many kinds of food and drinks. In the middle of the colors, I noticed one young lady wearing a black maxiskirt and a white shirt. To learn about her culture, I asked her, "Where are you from?" She gave me the answer to my previous question. She replied with a big smile, "I am from my parents, just like you". I said to myself, "Exactly, going from our parents to grandparents to ancestors, we all end up being from Adam (as) created by Allah (SWT)". So, why was love stronger than the cultural differences for those new couples in New York City? I have the answer from Allah (SWT), as He says:

"And one of His signs is that He created for you spouses from among yourselves so that you may find comfort in them. And

He has placed between you compassion and mercy. Surely this is a sign for people who reflect"

(Quran 30:21).

I also realized that the practice of faith varies widely, which I noticed in detail from visiting churches in New York City and Quebec City and shrines in Japan, and observing religious practices in those cities. It seemed that people from different religions were worshipping different Gods, but again, by reading the Holy Quran, Allah (SWT) comforted me by saying:

"O mankind, indeed, We have created you from male and female and made you peoples and tribes that you may know one another. Indeed, the most noble of you in the sight of Allah is the most righteous of you. Indeed, Allah is Knowing and Acquainted"

(Quran 49:13)

Remembering my scientific research activities in those cities, I utilized diverse sources of scientific knowledge to interpret data from my lab experiments. The different mathematical models I used to analyze my lab data seemed different in their applications. However, I realized that they have a similar profound concept. I imagined that these scientific laws could belong to one fundamental principle. This supposition informed my spirituality and encouraged me to look for the hidden forces beyond the material world. To find an answer, I tried to make an analogy between the mathematical models used in my lab experiments and my life experiences with people of different cultures. I said to myself, "People behave differently (because of different cultures) for the same human needs as they all belong to One Creator (SWT). In the same way, all the mathematical models I used to interpret my lab data look different because they belong to different fields of natural sciences (like different cultures). However, they also could belong to one Divine Science imposed by Allah (SWT) on the whole universe".

In conclusion, my current knowledge and perception have led me to conclude that spirituality is needed in Islam to be able to perceive that Allah (SWT) alone governs everything behind the stage of the visible material world. For my part, I realize now that the hidden Hand of Allah (SWT) was guiding me through every event of my life, whether positive or negative. At times, this has created beneficial opportunities in my life and has also steered me away from potentially harmful situations or choices.

Zin Eddine Dadach
Abu Dhabi, November 2025.

About the book

"All praise is for Allah alone, Who created the heavens and the earth, and brought into being light and darkness, and yet those who have rejected the call of the Truth ascribe others to be equals to their Lord (1). He is the one who created you from clay and specified a term [for you] and another fixed time, known only to Him; yet still you doubt! (2)"

(Quran 6:1-2)

The first part of this Quranic verse mentions that Allah (SWT) is the one who originated our planet Earth and the whole universe, while the second part indicates that Allah (SWT) is also our creator, as he created us from clay as part of Earth. Moreover, with his infinite mercy, He formed us with five senses to become aware of his creations in ourselves, and the universe, and he also gifted us a mind to ponder about the small part that we can sense. Indeed, we are one planet of many, one of many solar systems, one of many milky ways, one of many galaxies, all held in one universe. We can barely start to imagine the capacity of all this universe holds until we become overwhelmed by its mere complexity. It truly is extraordinary; there is so much our minds cannot gather, such is the beauty of Allah (SWT)'s creation.

"Praise be to Allah Who has revealed to His servant the Book devoid of all crookedness"

(Quran 18-1)

On the other hand, in this Quranic verse, it is Allah (SWT) who also sends down the Holy Quran as guidance for humanity. The Holy Quran is straightforward, that which has no bends and no corners to mystify people. Allah (SWT) speaks to us clearly and unambiguously to guide us to the straight path. The Holy Quran is classified into 30 chapters containing 114 Surahs (chapters), where each Surah contains many Ayat (verses). It should be noted that there are more than one thousand verses in the Holy Quran related to astronomy, cosmology, and natural sciences.

Finally, we could consider the Universe as an open Holy Quran and consider the Holy Quran as a Universe of knowledge and science.

> "*These are the Ayat (proofs, evidences, verses, lessons, revelations, etc.) of Allah, which We recite to you (O Muhammad SAW) with truth. Then, in which speech after Allah and His Ayat will they believe?*"
>
> (Quran 45:6)

The word "ayah' (Ayat in plural) and its derivatives are mentioned 382 times in the Quran. It has many different meanings. This book is about the signs of Allah (SWT) in the universe and also the Ayat we read from the Holy Quran. In fact, all the creations of Allah (SWT) in the universe and those mentioned in the Holy Quran are Ayat that show the Absolute Wisdom, Knowledge, and Power of the Creator (SWT). For example, a mobile phone is something that was put together in an organized way, so it would be rational to believe that it must have an organizer. In the same way, when we see the organization and the beauty in the universe and in our human body, isn't it rational to say that the universe has an organizer? To make us ponder, Allah (SWT) mentions some of His creations, such as winds, sun, moon, and stars in the Holy Quran. Indeed, the universe did not come into existence from nowhere. Allah (SWT) is undoubtedly the Creator as He (SWT) says:

> *"We shall show them our signs in the universe and within themselves until it becomes clear to them that the Quran is the Truth. Is it not enough that your lord is the witness of all things?"*

(Quran, 41:5).

The universe serves as Allah's classroom for humanity. Just as He established divine laws in the Quran to create social harmony, Allah embedded corresponding laws throughout nature to maintain cosmic balance. This parallel between revealed guidance and natural order demonstrates the unity of divine wisdom across spiritual and physical realms, encouraging Muslims to study both revelation and creation as complementary sources of knowledge. Therefore, we will be at peace with our souls and enjoy harmony in our societies and with nature only if we behave like the universe by obeying all the Divine Laws decreed by Allah (SWT) in the Holy Quran and Sunnah.

The Creator (SWT)

"In the Name of God, the Gracious, the Merciful.

1. Say, "He is God, the One.

2. God, the Absolute.

3. He begets not, nor was He begotten.

4. And there is none comparable to Him."

(Quran 112:1-4)

"Allah (SWT) is the Arabic name for God, derived from Al-Ilāh. Similar words exist in Hebrew (El) and Aramaic (Ellah). The first pillar of Islamic faith is believing that Allah (SWT) is the Divine Power who created us and the universe. True belief means more than acknowledging His existence—it means recognizing that He controls all affairs and movements in creation. Therefore, as a true believer, one should have a perfect understanding of the nature of Allah (SWT)'s divine existence. For this purpose, Allah (SWT) describes Himself to us through His Ninety-Nine Beautiful Names in the Noble Quran and the Prophet (SAW)'s sayings to glorify Him and worship Him as He deserves. To know the Beautiful Names of our Creator is, therefore, more critical and urgent than everything else in our lives.

The universe overflows with signs pointing to His existence. When we contemplate stars billions of light-years away, we witness "The

Magnificent." A mother's tender smile while cradling her newborn reflects "The Most Loving." Ocean waves thundering against cliffsides echo "The All-Strong." Spring's breathtaking beauty offers a glimpse of Paradise through "Lord of Majesty and Generosity." Even winter's bitter cold and summer's scorching heat remind us of "The Reckoner" and the reality of divine justice.

Furthermore, according to the Noble Quran: "Verily they are enemies to me except the Lord. Who has created me and it is He Who guides me. And it is He who feeds me and gives me to drink. And when I am ill, it is He who cures me." (Quran; 51:58), we should be very thankful to Allah (SWT) because He not only guides us through life with the Noble Quran and The Prophet (PBUH) but also provides everything to all living creatures. His provision knows no limits. He grants us material sustenance like food, water, shelter, and protection, while also nourishing our hearts with love through our families. He delights us with nature's beauty: vibrant flowers, gentle creatures, and fruits of countless flavors, shapes, and colors. In return for these countless blessings, He asks only for our gratitude, expressed through love for Him and kindness toward all His creation. The study of Allah (SWT)'s Beautiful Names and Attributes is therefore a matter of utmost importance for Muslims. The Quran's emphasis on mercy becomes clear through repetition: Al-Rahim (The All-Merciful) appears 227 times, Al-Rahman (The All-Compassionate) 170 times, and Al-Ghafur (The Forgiver) 91 times. This frequency reveals Allah's desire for us to know Him through His mercy above all. Moreover, several Quranic verses mention two different attributes of Allah (SWT). Some of these verses are:

'Know that God is Mighty and Wise' (Quran 2:209)

'Know that Allah is Rich and Praised' (Quran 2:267)

'Know that God is All-Hearing, All-Knowing'

(Quran 2: 244)

Understanding His Beautiful Names reveals our very purpose in existence. To ignore their profound meanings is to lose sight of why we were created. Each Beautiful Name we comprehend deepens our faith and draws us closer to our Creator. There is therefore nothing more sacred and blessed than understanding the meaning of the Beautiful Names of Allah (SWT) and, most importantly, living by them. For example, learning the meaning of His Beautiful Name "The All-Merciful, will guide us to show mercy to all His creatures. Moreover, knowing the meaning of the Beautiful Names of Allah (SWT) allows us to thank Him for all that He has provided us to make our life comfortable, to trust Him (Tawakkul) when we need help to solve our daily problems, and therefore fulfil our divine duties of justice and charity with love and thankfulness. To discover some characteristics of our Creator (SWT), a short description of some of the Beautiful Names of Allah (SWT) is given in this chapter.

The Creator

"He is Allah, the Creator, the Producer, the Fashioner; to Him belong the best names. Whatever is in the heavens and Earth is exalting Him. And He is the Exalted in Might, the Wise."

(Quran 59:24)

Al-Khaliq (The Creator) appears eight times in the Holy Quran, each mention reminding us of His unique power. While humans can only reshape existing materials, Allah creates from absolute nothingness. Our abilities have limits; His creative power knows no bounds. Every atom, every star, every heartbeat exists only by His Will. Every one of Allah's creations has its beginning with Him, and He gave it its form according to His Divine Knowledge as indicated in this Quranic verse:

"For verily it is thy Lord who is the Master-Creator, knowing all things"

(Quran 15:86).

Moreover, mankind has been gifted with the best natural powers and qualities which other creatures have not been endowed with as Allah (SWT) says *"Indeed, We created humans in the best form." (Qur'an 95:4).* This verse reveals three complementary aspects of divine creation: Al-Khaliq (The Creator), Al-Bari (The Producer), and Al-Musawwir (The Fashioner). Consider how a house comes into being: someone must conceive the idea, another must construct it, and yet another must give it beautiful form. Allah (SWT) perfectly embodies all three roles in every act of creation. First, He is Al-Khaliq, the Creator, who conceives and brings forth from nothingness. Second, He is Al-Bari, the Producer, who initiates and gives existence. Finally, He is Al-Musawwir, The Fashioner, who shapes and gives form to His creation.

The All-Knowing & The Most Wise

Al-Aleem (The All-Knowing) graces the Quran 157 times, with variations appearing 17 more times. This frequency reveals how central divine knowledge is to our understanding of Allah. His knowledge encompasses all time: past, present, and future exist as one before Him. He sees not only our outward actions but also reads the secret intentions of our hearts. Before Him, nothing remains hidden.

"The Most Wise" (Al-Hakeem) means He possesses perfect judgment, discerning right from wrong with flawless understanding. His designs in nature and life are flawless and purposeful. He alone qualifies to judge the true worth of all things, as He says

"And Allah is your protector, and He is the All-Knowing, the Most Wise"

(Qur'an 66:2).

Therefore, understanding Allah (SWT) as both All-Knowing and Most Wise brings peace to the believer. We trust His plan for us completely, knowing He makes no mistakes. Even if we cannot perceive the Wisdom of His decrees in this life, we know the benefit will be revealed on the Day of Judgment. This is the Mercy of Allah (SWT), the All-Knowing, the All-Wise.

The King, The Ruler, The Owner of Dominion

The Beautiful Names of Allah (SWT) Malik, Maalik, and Maleek all come from the root "maa-laa-kaa", which points to three main meanings. The first main meaning is that He has possession and ownership. The second is that He has power and ability, and the third main meaning is that He has control and authority. This emphasizes His complete independence from all creation. Even if every human heart turned away from Him in disbelief, He would remain the absolute King. His dominion suffers no diminishment, not even by a gnat's wing, as Allah (SWT) declares:

> "So exalted is Allah, the Sovereign, the Truth; there is no deity except Him, Lord of the Noble Throne."
>
> (Quran 23:116).

So, if we seek refuge, we should turn to Him because only He can provide relief. A believer who knows that he (she) has Allah (SWT) is free from worldly desires and worries and can find happiness only by being close to The Sovereign. He will then focus on how to fulfil his divine obligations of justice and charity with love and thankfulness.

The All-Powerful

None other than Him has any kind of independent power. If any power is found with anyone or anything, it is by the permission of Allah

(SWT). No one can claim to have a power 'other than His Power.' Every conceivable power exists and subsists by His Power as indicated in this Quranic verse:

"Say, 'O Allah, Owner of Sovereignty, You give sovereignty to whom You will, and You take it away from whom You will. You honor whom You will and You humble whom You will. In Your hand is [all] good. Indeed, You are over all things competent."

(Qur'an 3:26).

When The Creator (SWT) wills something into existence, He simply commands "Be!" and it instantly becomes reality, as the Quran states: *"Verily, His command, when He intends a thing, is only that He says to it, 'Be!' and it is!"* (Quran 36:82). This profound truth offers hope to every believer: when we need something from Allah, we must submit completely to Him and strengthen our relationship with our Creator.

The Sustainer & The Bestower

Allah (SWT) is Ar-Razzaq, the Sustainer, who provides nourishment for all His creatures. He creates the means for growth in body, soul, and mind. Similar to this is the name Al-Wahhab, The Bestower, which highlights Allah's (SWT) boundless generosity. His gifts require nothing in return. Ar-Razzaq (The Sustainer) operates on two levels. First, He provides material sustenance, but unlike simple gifts, this often requires our effort and striving. Second, and more importantly, He nourishes our hearts, faith, and souls with spiritual sustenance. While material wealth fades with time, spiritual nourishment carries

11

eternal value. Allah (SWT) has predetermined our sustenance, but this knowledge is hidden from us. Therefore, we should strive through good deeds and prayer, trusting in Allah's (SWT) provision: *"And in heaven is your sustenance, as (also) that which ye are promised" (Quran 51:22).* Therefore, for true peace, we should find contentment in Allah's gifts, as the Prophet (SAW) taught:

> *"Whoever among you wakes up physically healthy, feeling safe and secure within himself, with food for the day, it is as if he acquired the whole world."*

> [Hasan (Darussalam) Sunan Ibn Majah 4141]

The Just

Al-Hakam (SWT), The Just, corrects matters and ensures fairness with perfect equity. Justice is His Divine Attribute – He is just in word, action, and judgment. As the Quran states:

> *"And the word of your Lord has been fulfilled in truth and in justice. None can alter His words, and He is the Hearing, the Knowing"*

> (Qur'an 6:115).

Indeed, Allah (SWT) delivers absolute justice with flawless wisdom. He gives each their due and maintains perfect order within His creation. Because Allah embodies perfect justice, He calls us to mirror this quality:

"Indeed, Allah orders justice and good conduct and giving to relatives and forbids immorality and bad conduct and oppression. He admonishes you that perhaps you will be reminded"

(Quran 16:90).

Divine justice becomes our moral compass.

Living with Allah's Presence

True faith means living with the constant awareness of Allah (SWT)'s presence:

"And He is with you (by His knowledge) wheresoever you may be"

(Quran; 57:4).

Indeed, when we act, He is "The All-Seeing"; when we speak, He is "The All-Hearing"; even our thoughts are known to Him, "The All-Knowing". This awareness, coupled with His attribute as "The Reckoner", inspires believers to avoid wrongdoing as Allah (SWT) says:

"So, whosoever does good equal to the weight of an atom (or a small ant) shall see it. And whosoever does evil equal to the weight of an atom (or a small ant) shall see it"

(Quran; 99:7-8).

Finally, as mentioned in this Quranic verse:

13

"They have no protector other than Him, and He makes none to share in His Decision and His rule"

(Quran; 18:26),

we should worship Him alone because He is the "The Protecting Associate" of the believers. The Prophet Muhammad (SAW) promised us:

"Allah has ninety-nine Beautiful Names, and whoever knows their meaning will enter Paradise"

[Sahih Bukhari].

This hadith transforms our study of these Names from an academic exercise into a pathway to eternal bliss.

Spirituality in Islam

Islamic spirituality weaves seamlessly through every moment of daily life. At its heart lies the quest to connect with Allah (SWT), drawing closer to our Creator through worship, contemplation, and reflection. This spiritual journey extends far beyond ritual obligations to encompass a sincere, transformative relationship with Allah (SWT) that illuminates every aspect of our existence.

> *"We created man from sounding clay, from mud moulded into shape..."*
>
> (Quran 15:26).

This Quranic verse reveals that Allah (SWT) fashioned Adam (as) from clay, establishing humanity's profound connection to Earth itself. The Prophet (SAW) beautifully explained this divine design: *"Allah Almighty created Adam from a handful taken from the earth, so the children of Adam reflect the earth's diversity. They come with different skin colors and textures, embodying the earth's varied nature: smooth and rough, fertile and barren"* [Sunan al-Tirmidhī 2955]. Moreover, like animals, human beings have been created weak with physiological and psychological needs to be moving and social creatures on Earth. These needs include food, water, air, sleep, sex, love, and security. Human beings and animals also share five physical senses – sight, touch, hearing, taste, and smell – that allow us to perceive and react to the world around us.

Gift of Reason and Wisdom

What distinguishes humans from all other creatures is the divine gift of reason. While animals follow instinct, Adam (as) received the precious faculty of intellect (Al-Aql). The Quran emphasizes this blessing:

> *"And they will say: Had we but listened or used our intelligence, we should not have been among dwellers of the blazing fire"*
>
> (Quran 67:10).

This extraordinary mind bestows upon us remarkable capabilities:

1. Choice: We can make conscious decisions based on reason and understanding.

2. Information Retention: We can learn and store knowledge for future use.

3. Reasoning: We can analyze information, draw conclusions, and solve problems.

4. Coordinating Brain Messages: We can integrate information from various senses and experiences to form a comprehensive understanding,

Moreover, building upon this foundation of reason, human beings can achieve wisdom. Wisdom involves applying logic and reasoning to reach sound conclusions. The Quran emphasizes the importance of wisdom:

"He grants wisdom to whoever He wills. And whoever is granted wisdom is certainly blessed with a great privilege. But none will be mindful ˈof thisˈ except people of reason"

(Quran 2:269).

As a great privilege, people gifted with wisdom will be able to perceive the signs of Allah (SWT) in their own body and the universe to help them to think about life after death, to differentiate between the good and evil, justice and unfairness, freedom, and domination, the moral and immoral, and to understand the purpose of this life.

After forming Adam (as) from clay and granting him intellect, Allah (SWT) commanded the angels:

"When it is properly shaped and I have blown My Spirit into it, you should then bow down in prostration"

(Quran 15:29).

Notice how Allah (SWT) calls the soul "My Spirit," revealing the extraordinary honor He bestowed upon humanity. This divine attribution elevates the human soul above all creation. Since Adam (as) has been given the honor of being in closeness with the Divine, it came to be the object of prostration by the angels. It should also be noted that Allah (SWT) did not give us enough knowledge to understand our souls. Indeed, when The Prophet (SAW) was asked about the nature of the soul, Allah (SWT) instructed him to answer them as: *"They ask you ˈO Prophetˈ about the soul. Say:*

17

Its nature is known only to my Lord, and you ˋO humanityˋ have been given but little knowledge"

(Quran 17:85).

Once we realize that we were created as well as the whole universe by a Divine Power called Allah (SWT), we start contemplating nature and the universe to perceive His signs and follow His Book (The Holy Quran) and Sunnah in order to worship Him in this short life to deserve Eternity in His Paradise.

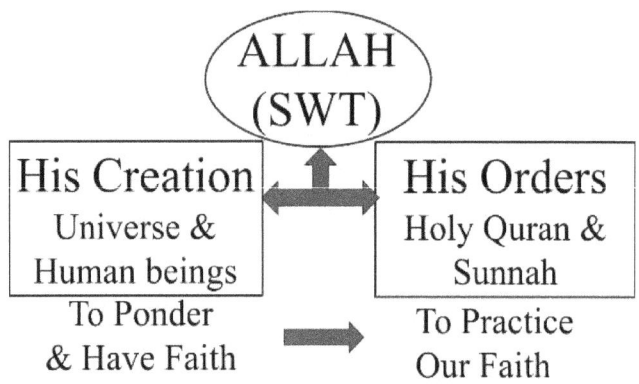

Since humans possess both body and soul, Islam's core worship practices engage our complete being. Prayer, fasting, zakat, and Hajj unite physical actions with spiritual devotion, creating a holistic path to Allah (SWT). Each act of worship nourishes both dimensions of our humanity.

Prayer (Salah): Salah (Prayer): The very word 'Salah' stems from 'silah,' meaning connection, revealing prayer's true purpose: forging a spiritual bridge between servant and Creator. While our bodies move through standing, bowing, and prostrating, our souls engage through Khushu, that sacred state of focused devotion, humility, and complete surrender to Allah (SWT). During prayer, Khushuu involves concentrating on the meaning of the Quran being recited, feeling a sense of awe and love for Allah (SWT), and minimizing distractions. The Prophet Muhammad (SAW) said:

"When anyone of you is engaged in the Prayer, he is holding an intimate conversation with his Lord."

[Muslim].

He also said:

"The best prayer is the one in which there is the most Khushuu"
[Sahih al-Bukhari].

Therefore, the Prophet (SAW) took his prayer as a source of tranquility. Indeed, when telling Bilal (ra) to pronounce the adhan (call to prayer), he said,

"O Bilal, give us rest with it."

[Abu Dawud].

Fasting (Sawm): While the physical act of fasting involves abstaining from food and drink and other wrongdoings, the soul benefits by developing self-discipline, empathy for the less fortunate, and a deeper appreciation for Allah's (SWT) blessings.

19

Zakat (Almsgiving): The physical action involves giving a portion of one's wealth to charity. This will create harmony in societies and good relationships between the poor and the rich. The soul is also purified through generosity, compassion, and fulfilling a religious obligation.

Hajj (Pilgrimage): Hajj involves a series of physical actions performed at specific locations in Mecca. The soul's journey focuses on self-reflection, sacrifice, and achieving spiritual unity with fellow Muslims around the planet.

"We showed him the Way: whether he be grateful or ungrateful (rests on his will)" (Quran 76:3).

During these religious practices and our daily activities, our bodies have earthly desires, while our souls yearn for connection with Allah (SWT). By their animal nature and needs (body), human beings look for material perfection to enjoy all the material pleasures and bounties of the world. According to this Quranic verse, this inner struggle stems from the free will Allah (SWT) has given us.

"Indeed, We offered the trust to the heavens and the earth and the mountains, but they ˈallˈ declined to bear it, being fearful of it. But humanity assumed it, ˈforˈ they are truly wrongful ˈto themselvesˈ and ignorant ˈof the consequencesˈ"

(Quran 33:72)

Before entering this world, humanity accepted the sacred trust (Amanah) mentioned in this verse. In return, Allah (SWT) appointed us as His vicegerents (Khalifa) on Earth. With this honour comes both power and responsibility: we must fulfil our divine obligations (Takleef) of justice and charity in every aspect of our lives, whether social or professional. From my own understanding, since Allah (SWT) (Divine) controls the universe (material), we will perform all our divine duties with love and thankfulness only if our soul (from His Spirit) controls our body's desires (material). He then asks us to be patient while obeying His orders. For example, Allah (SWT) created us with an inclination to money. At the same time, He asks us to use money with no exaggeration and give part of it to the needy as charity.

Ibad Al Rahman (The true servants)

"The true servants (Ibad) of the Most Compassionate (AL Rahman) are those who walk on the Earth humbly, and when the ignorant address them 'improperly', they only respond with peace

(Quran 25:63)

Your journey to becoming true servants (Ibad Al-Rahman) begins with faith (Iman) in the Creator. As Allah (SWT) declares: *"Indeed, within the heavens and Earth are signs for the believers"* (Quran 45:3). This verse calls us to recognize that creation itself testifies to Allah's absolute sovereignty. Every sunrise, every heartbeat, every grain of sand speaks of the One who alone governs the universe. Therefore, seeking His Pleasure is the aim of all our personal and professional activities. Moreover, only His Commands (Quran and Sunnah) should constitute

21

the laws to follow during our lives. The stronger and deeper this conviction, the more profound the faith will be, and it will enable us to walk the path of spirituality with patience and persistence and using our body's desires based only on His instructions and guidance as Allah (SWT) says:

> "and who is more erring than he who follows his low desires without any guidance from Allah?"
>
> (Quran 28:50)

> "And if you obey Him, you will be [rightly] guided "
>
> (Quran 24:54).

The second stage of spirituality in Islam is of obedience (Tara). To be guided, a human being should deprive himself of selfishness and admit subservience to Allah (SWT) in practice after having proclaimed faith in Him as his Creator. Thus, it means that a Muslim should not only acknowledge Allah (SWT) as his Lord and Sovereign but should submit before Him and make his entire life in obedience to the Lord of the universe, following the orders in The Holy Quran and Sunnah.

> "People, worship your Lord who created you and those who lived before you, so that you may become pious
>
> (Quran 2:21).

The third stage of spirituality is piety (Taqwa) which is the goal of worship Allah (SWT). The Arabic word Taqwa (piety, fear, or mindfulness) has its origin from the word "prevention' to avoid His punishment. Therefore, Taqwa consists in taking all preventive steps to stay away from everything which Allah (SWT) has forbidden or even that which he dislikes even slightly, and taking all steps to obey all that Allah (SWT) has ordered.

> *"Allah commands justice, (Ihsan) the doing of good, and liberality to kith and kin, and He forbids all shameful deeds, and injustice and rebellion: He instructs you, that you may receive admonition"*
>
> (Quran 16:90).

The final and the top stage of spirituality of the true servant is benediction (Ihsan). To explain the importance of Ihsan, the Prophet (SAW) said: "Ihsan is to worship Allah (SWT) as though you see Him, and if you cannot see Him, then indeed He sees you" [al-Ṣamt li Ibn Abī Dunyā 22]. We can understand from this that Ihsan means to do every act of worship and good deed and avoid every evil action in the best possible manner, as if we see Allah (SWT) in front of us. Moreover, Ihsan (excellence) will also encourage us to achieve superiority during all our professional or social activities, like doing our job at its best, have good relationship and taking care of people and all creatures around us. For this, the will of the true servant in this life should always be in concordance with the Will of Allah (SWT). For example, when Aishah (ra) was asked about the character of the Prophet (SAW), she said

23

"His character was the Quran"

[Bukhārī, al-Adab al-Mufrad, 308].

Indeed, he was like a walking Quran during all his interactions with people and animals, and his sayings. Therefore, Allah (SWT) advises us to follow the Prophet (SAW) as He says in the Quranic verse:

"Indeed, in the Messenger of Allah (Muhammad SAW), you have a good example to follow for him who hopes in (the Meeting with) Allah and the Last Day and remembers Allah much

(Quran 33:21)

Moreover, to deserve the pleasure of Allah (SWT), believers should not only do good deeds but convince others to follow them. At the same time, they should not only avoid the evils but invite people around them to do the same, as Allah (SWT) says:

"You are the best community ever raised for humanity as you encourage good, forbid evil, and believe in Allah"

(Quran 3:110).

In this path of spirituality, a person will become Mu'min (faithful), Muslim (obedient), Muttaqi (pious), and Muhsin (beneficent). In conclusion, a person who reaches this state attains the highest summit of spirituality and is nearest to Allah (SWT) as He says,

"Allah has promised the believing men and believing women gardens beneath which rivers flow, wherein they abide eternally, and pleasant dwellings in gardens of perpetual residence; but approval from Allah is greater. It is that which is the great attainment"

(Quran 9:72)

Love and Protection of Allah (SWT)

"O you who have believed, whoever of you should revert from his religion – Allah will bring forth [in place of them] people He will love them and they will love Him"

(Quran 5:54)

Besides the five obligations, Muslims can perform supererogatory worship (Al Nawafeel) as extra prayers during the day, fasting every Monday and Thursday, giving voluntary charity (Sadaqah), and performing a voluntary pilgrimage (Umrah). These voluntary acts of worship will lead us to the Love and Protection of Allah (SWT) as indicated in this Prophet (SAW)'s saying: "Allah (SWT) said: Whoever is hostile to an ally of Mine, I have declared war upon him, and when my servant approaches Me with anything more beloved to Me than what I have made obligatory upon him, and he continues to do so. My servant draws near to Me by performing voluntary acts of worship until I love him. If I love him, I will be his hearing with which he hears, his sight with which he sees, and his hand with which he strikes, and his leg with which he walks, and if he asks Me, I will give

25

him, and if he seeks Me for protection, I will protect him, and I do not hesitate from anything more than taking the soul of my faithful servant, he hates death and I hate to hurt him." [Al-Bukhari Hadith 25, 40 Hadith Qudsi].

Ulul Al Albab: Intelligent servants

> *"And they reflect on the creation of the heavens and the Earth 'and pray Our Lord! You have not created 'all of' this without purpose. Glory be to You! Protect us from the torment of the Fire"*
>
> (Quran 3:191)

Some characteristics of intelligent servants (Ulul Albab) can be found in these six Quranic verses:

> *(1) to sincerely seek, explore, understand, and discover the secrets of science and knowledge taught by Allah (SWT)*
>
> (Quran 3:191)

> *(2) to be willing to transfer his knowledge to others to improve social conditions and willing to give warning*
>
> (Quran 14:52),

> *(3) to stand up for the right after telling them apart from the wrong*
>
> (Quran 5:100)

(4) to be critical about incoming information and make sure it is true

(Quran 39:18)

(5) to act mindfully and always take lesson from the history of the past ummahs

(6) to not fear other than Allah (SWT).

To reach this spiritual status, the Prophet (SAW) is our example to follow for his emotional intelligence. His exquisite character, his sensitivity, his ability to acknowledge his own and others' emotions, as mentioned by Allah (SWT)

"And you are a man of great moral character"

(Quran 68:4).

Indeed, The Prophet's every word was wrapped with kindness and tenderness. In the situations that required firmness, he demonstrated it, but with tact and wisdom. When The Prophet (SAW) would come across a difficult situation, He instantly turned to his Lord in prayer. When the Prophet (SAW) needed guidance, Allah (SWT) sent him revelation (Wahy). These are two hadiths that we can use as lessons from the Prophet (SAW):

Strive for that which will benefit you, seek the help of Allah, and do not feel helpless. If anything befalls you, do not say, "if only I had done such and such" rather say, "Allah has decreed and whatever he wills, He does." Saying 'If' opens (the door) to the deeds of Satan"

[Sunan Ibn Majah 79]

"Make things easy and do not make things difficult. Give glad tidings and do not frighten them away."

[Sahiḥ Muslim 1733].

"This ˹Quran˺ is a ˹sufficient˺ message for humanity so that they may take it as a warning and know that there is only One God, and so that people of reason may be mindful"

(Quran 14:52).

In conclusion, spiritual journey is related to the teachings of the Quran and Sunnah that incorporate spiritual consciousness into a system of belief, worship, morality, and social responsibility. It engages the human soul, intellect, and needs in a dynamic movement of spiritual purification, character improvement, and moral perfection. This is brought about by establishing Allah (SWT) at the very center of every spiritual pursuit in such a way that spiritual intelligence would have spiritual and rational resonance with the Divine while sustaining a spiritually positive, balanced, and transparent transformation of the self and environment.

Power of Sujud

"Only those believe in Our sign who, when they are reminded of them, fall down prostrate, and glorify the Praises of their Lord, and they are not proud"

(Quran 32:15)

On the last note, how to be the closest to Allah (SWT) during our prayers and feel His Love and Mercy? Based on this Quranic verse, The All-Wise (SWT) commands the frontal lobe to be placed on the ground in prostration (Sujud). During this time of sujud, the prostration of the heart is in its humility (khushu), such that a person could physically rise from prostration, yet the heart would still be performing sujud.

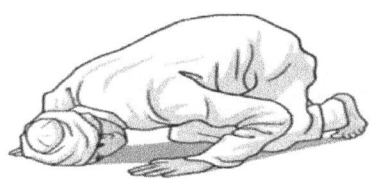

In this topic, the Prophet (SAW) said, "The nearest a slave can be to his Lord is while they are prostrating, so increase in supplication" [Ṣaḥīḥ Muslim, Musnad Aḥmad]. Since every order from Allah (SWT) is only to guide us for what is best of us, I asked myself, "Why prostration?" This is what I have learned: The human brain consists of four main lobes: (1) the frontal lobe, (2) the occipital lobe, (3) the

29

temporal lobe, and (4) the parietal lobe. Each lobe has its own special function, while at the same time working together and supplementing one another. The frontal lobe of human beings is different than that of animals because it has centers for speech and behavior. Moreover, the dimension of the frontal lobe compared to the other parts of the brain is what separates human beings from other animals. For human beings, the frontal lobe is almost 40% of the entire brain. For apes and chimpanzees, it is about 15% to 17%. For dogs, it's 7% and for cats, 3.5%. The prefrontal cortex is the main unit for building the character of a person. It plays a role in both initiative and judgment. In fact, the Frontal lobe is the CEO of the brain. The rest of the brain is just past programming. Therefore, by putting our forehead on the ground during Sujud, we are messaging the CEO to start wiring new connections and commanding to bring forth the best version of us.

"And thus did We show Abraham the realm of the heavens and the earth that he would be among the certain [in faith]"

(Quran 6: 75)

Our Creator Allah (SWT) is the Creator of the whole universe as He describes Himself to us with His Beautiful Names. I have tried to present some of His Names in this first part of the book which is also related to our spiritual journey to draw us closer to Him and benefit from His Love and Mercy. Finally, and as mentioned in this Quranic verse, the ultimate goal of our spiritual journey is to feel with the complete conviction and certitude without any smallest doubt (Yaqueen) the presence of our Creator, as Prophet Moses (AS) said:

No! Indeed, my Lord is with me; He will guide me" (Quran 42: 62) and our Prophet (SAW) said "Do not grieve; indeed, Allah (SWT) is with us"

(Quran 9: 40).

Divine Forces & Divine Laws

"It is Allah who erected the heavens without pillars that you [can] see; then He established Himself above the Throne and made subject the sun and the moon, each running [its course] for a specified term. He arranges [each] matter; He details the signs that you may, of the meeting with your Lord, be certain."

(Quran 13:2)

Having established the certainty that Allah (SWT) created our universe, we now explore how He governs all creation through His infinite wisdom, power, and mercy. This section reveals the divine forces and laws that operate throughout the cosmos, their signs clearly evident in numerous Quranic verses. Our ultimate goal remains unchanged: to witness Allah's perfect Oneness (Tawhid) reflected in every phenomenon across the universe.

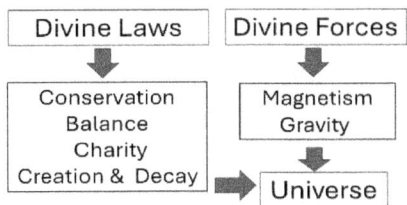

As shown in this figure, Allah (SWT) rules the universe with his Divine Forces and Divine Laws. Now, since humankind accepted the trust (Amanah),

"And then the Record of their deeds shall be placed before them, and you will see the guilty full of fear for what it contains and will say: "Woe to us! What a Record this is! It leaves nothing, big or small, but encompasses it." They will find their deeds confronting them. Your Lord wrongs no one.

(Quran 18:49).

"To Allah belongs all power, and Allah will strongly enforce the penalty"

(Quran 2:165)

Regarding the existence of the Divine Forces and the Dinie Laws, the Holy Quran has revealed to us one of the greatest truths of existence, which is that

"All power belongs to Allah" (Quran 2:165); that "There is no power except with Allah"

(Quran 18:39)

and that Allah is "the Possessor of strength, the Sturdy"

(Quran 51:58)

There are also many other Quranic verses related the divine forces, and the divine laws present in the universe which we enjoy reading, but we do not pay attention to them.

Two fundamental divine forces govern our universe: Earth's gravity and its magnetic field. Though science has studied these forces extensively, they operate only by Allah's permission. This divine control extends to every force and law throughout creation, including those within our own bodies.

> *"Allah is He Who raised the heavens without any pillars that ye can see; is firmly established on the throne (of authority); He has subjected the sun and the moon (to his Law)! Each one runs (its course) for a term appointed. He doth regulate all affairs, explaining the signs in detail, that ye may believe with certainty in the meeting with your Lord"*
>
> (Quran 13:2)

The phrase "without any pillars you see" points to invisible divine forces: gravity and electromagnetism. These forces orchestrate the cosmic dance, enabling celestial bodies to interact and move in perfect harmony. What appears as empty space actually pulses with divine energy. The various movements caused by the various interacting forces have created a dynamic balance between the celestial bodies. As mentioned in this Quranic verse, the celestial bodies rise high in the upper space, and this is a clear manifestation of the power of Allah (SWT).

Gravity

> *"Verily! Allah grasps the heavens and the earth lest they move away from their places (orbits), and if they were to move away*

from their places, there is not one that could grasp them after
Him. Truly, He is Ever Most Forbearing, Oft Forgiving"

(Quran 35:41)

The divine gravitational force is an invisible force that pulls things according to their size. The larger the size, the more gravitational force it has, and it attracts others to it. This Quranic verse is clearly a sign that Allah (SWT) uses the divine force of gravity that holds the planets in their orbits.

"Did we not make the earth a receptacle (kifatan)?"

(Quran 77:25)

Earth's gravity performs countless miracles: anchoring all creatures to the ground, enabling rainfall, and even allowing us to breathe. Without gravitational force, life itself would be impossible. Every breath we take depends on Allah's grace working through gravity, which holds oxygen molecules within our atmosphere. Indeed, in this Quranic verse, Allah (SWT) is informing us about the force of gravity that makes Earth a receptacle or container for the living as well as for a resting place. Indeed, the Arabic word for receptacle used in this Quranic verse is "kifatan". The word "kifatan" is derived from the verb "ka-fa-ta" which literally means to attract or to grab something or to bind it.

"It is He Who created the night and the day, and the sun and
the moon. Each of them is floating in its orbit"

(Quran 21:33)

Moreover, the Divine Force of Gravity also keeps planets in their orbits around the sun. Indeed, the sun, being the most massive object in the solar system, exerts a strong gravitational pull on all the planets. Finally, it is important to notice that Allah (SWT) created the planets at initial speeds, and because of the force of the sun's gravity, the planets remain in their elliptical orbits around the sun as indicated in this Quranic verse.

> "Allah is He Who created you in (a state of) weakness, then gave you strength after weakness, then, after strength, gave (you) weakness and grey hair. He creates what He wills. And it is He Who is the All-Knowing, the All-Powerful (i.e. Able to do all things)"
>
> (Quran 30:54)

As stated in this Quranic verse, in the same way that Allah (SWT) created the universe under several divine forces to be subservient to humankind, He also gave us some physical and mental strength to fulfill our social, professional, and religious duties. However, unlike the universe, which is governed by the divine forces, human beings have the freedom to use their physical and mental forces as they wish.

> "Shake the trunk of the palm-tree towards yourself and fresh and ripe dates shall fall upon you".
>
> (Quran 19:25)

As an example of our physical strength and the existence of the divine force of gravity, the story of Mary (as) in this Quranic verse. Indeed, with Allah (SWT) 's permission, Mary (as) used her physical force to shake the tree, and the effect desired by Allah (SWT) was that dates would fall from the tree by Earth's gravity.

Now, from the theoretical point of view, the force of gravity is defined in scientific textbooks as a fundamental interaction that causes mutual attraction between all things that have mass. It is claimed in scientific textbooks that the divine force of gravity is a discovery made by Isaac Newton as he stated, "Every particle of matter in the universe attracts every other particle with a force that is directly proportional to the product of the mass of the particles and inversely proportional to the square of the distance between these particles".

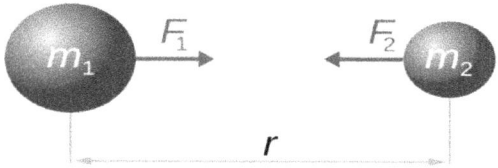

His statement was then expressed as a simple vector equation where m_1 and m_2 are the two masses separated by a distance r, and the gravitational force ($F_1 = F_2$) is defined as:

$$F_1 = F_2 = G \frac{m_1 . m_2}{r^2} \qquad (1)$$

More recently, Einstein defined Earth's gravity as curved space phenomenon and rejected Newton's Law of gravitation. Nowadays, scientists can still not answer the most basic question: why does gravity attract mass?

History reveals that Muslim scientist Ibn Al-Haytham discovered and documented the principles of gravity six centuries before Newton. He pioneered the scientific method while recognizing these as divine laws governing motion. This demonstrates how Islamic scholarship anticipated many so-called 'modern' discoveries. Al-Baghdadi's (lived in Baghdad 11th-12th centuries) also mentioned the laws related to free-falling objects. He claimed that when a body starts falling, a residue of aggressive preference still subsists in it and opposes the natural inclination (gravity) that causes the body to descend slowing down its fall. The increase of velocity of the fall is due to the gradual weakening of the aggressive inclination. This clearly shows that Al-Baghdadi spoke of the effect of the divine force of gravity. Another Muslim scientist also mentioned gravity is Al-Khazin in his book "Balance of Wisdom". This proves that Muslim scientists discovered gravity long time before Isaac Newton.

Magnetism

"Indeed, Allah does not do injustice, [even] as much as an atom's weight; while if there is a good deed, He multiplies it and gives from Himself a great reward"

(Quran 4:40)

The Quranic reference to "the weight of an atom" (dharrah) points to the smallest particles of matter, connecting us to the subatomic realm that modern physics has revealed. Within each atom exist three fundamental particles: protons, neutrons, and electrons, each playing a crucial role in creation's architecture. Protons are positively charged particles, found in the nucleus of an atom. Electrons are negatively charged particles and are also orbiting the nucleus of the atom in energy shells. While gravity governs planetary orbits, a different divine force operates at the atomic level. The Divine Force of Magnetism holds electrons in their paths around the nucleus. This occurs because the positively charged nucleus attracts the negatively charged electrons, creating the fundamental structure of all matter. The force acting on a charged particle due to electric and magnetic fields is known as the Lorentz force. This is used in electromagnetism and is also known as the electromagnetic force. Hendrick Lorentz derived in 1895 the modern formula as stated in Equation 2 below

$$F = q \ (E + v \ x \ B) \tag{2}$$

where F is the force acting on the particle, q is the electric charge of the particle, E is the external electric field, v is the velocity of the charge, B is the magnetic field and x is the cross-product operation defined for the vector quantities such that the magnetic force is guaranteed to remain perpendicular to both the velocity and the magnetic field. These quantities are depicted in the figure below.

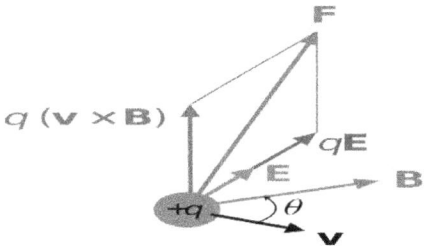

"And We also sent down iron in which there lies great force, and which has many uses for mankind"

Quran 57:25)

This verse reveals that Allah (SWT) sent iron down for humanity's benefit. Modern science discovers that Earth's magnetic field originates from electric currents flowing through iron alloys in our planet's core. These currents result from convection as heat escapes from the Earth's center, creating the protective magnetic shield around our world. A remarkable numerical sign emerges: this verse about iron appears as verse number 5100 in the Quran's sequence, precisely matching the depth of 5100 kilometers where iron concentrates in Earth's core. Subhan Allah! Such precision points beyond coincidence to divine design.

"And We made the sky a protected shield and they turn away from its sign"

(Quran 21:32)

It is also known nowadays that electrical currents generate the magnetic field with invisible lines of force flowing between Earth's magnetic poles. This verse describes Earth's protective systems: the visible atmosphere shields us from meteorites and debris, while the invisible magnetosphere deflects harmful cosmic radiation. Both work together as Allah's comprehensive protection for life on Earth.

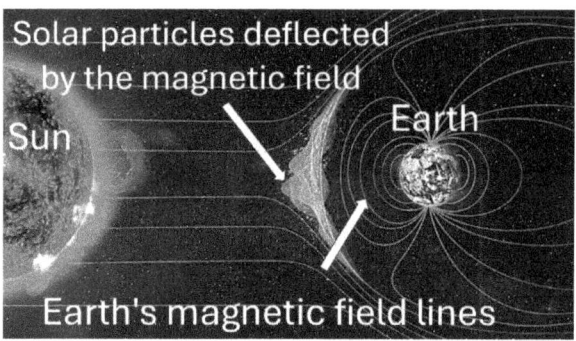

These electronic radiations travel faster than the speed of sound of up to 800 kilometers per second. When they collide with the Earth's magnetic field their speed would reduce below the speed of sound, cancelling their effectiveness. Scientists say that if it were not for the presence of this field in this area, life would have disappeared on Earth. Furthermore, magnetic fields surround not only Earth but also the sun and all galaxies. To this day, the origins of the Earth's magnetic field remain a mystery. A new study led by Oxford University and MIT has recovered a 3.7-billion-year record of Earth's magnetic field and found that it looks remarkably like the field surrounding Earth today. One possibility for this is that cosmic magnetism is primordial, tracing all the way back to the birth of the universe. In that case, weak magnetism is supposed to exist everywhere, even in the "voids" of the cosmic web, the very darkest, emptiest regions of the universe. The omnipresent magnetism would have seeded the stronger fields that blossomed in galaxies and clusters. This new scientific discovery is a clear indication of the Divine Law of Magnetism which is another great blessing from Allah (SWT).

> *"Unto Allah belong the East and the West, and whithersoever ye turn, there is Allah's Expression. Lo! Allah is All-Embracing, All-Knowing."*
>
> (Quran 2:115)

One of the benefits of the Earth's magnetism is the use of the compass. The compass is a device that indicates direction, and it is one of the most important tools used in navigation. A magnetic compass consists of a magnetized needle that rotates to align with the Earth's magnetic field, with its ends pointing to what are known as the magnetic north pole and the magnetic south pole. While Greeks and Chinese understood magnetic properties, Muslim scientists pioneered their practical application by creating the first compass. This innovation transformed navigation and exemplifies how Islamic scholars advanced from theoretical knowledge to beneficial technology. This was done by rubbing the needle on a magnet, then placing it over a container of water where it floats on two small wooden sticks, so that the needle points towards the magnetic north. The first reference to the appearance of an iron compass in the form of a fish in the Islamic world was in a Persian novel in the year 1232. The first Arabic reference to a compass in the form of a magnetic needle in a container of water came from the Yemeni sultan and astronomer Al-Ashraf in the year 1282. He also appears to have been the first to use the compass for astronomical purposes. In 1475 AD, the oceanographer Ibn Majid invented the first needle that sat on a tooth so that it could move freely without the need for a water container, as was customary in the past and as mentioned in his book Al-Fawa'id".

"We have certainly seen the turning of your face, [O Muhammad], toward the heaven, and We will surely turn you to a qiblah with which you will be pleased. So turn your face toward al-Masjid al-Haram. And wherever you [believers] are, turn your faces toward it [in prayer]"

(Quran 2:144).

The Qibla compass represents Islamic scientific innovation serving spiritual needs. In the fourteenth century, astronomer Ibn al-Shatir created a remarkable device combining a universal sundial with a magnetic compass, allowing Muslims to determine both prayer times and the direction of Mecca. He invented this compass to determine the direction to Mecca and the prayer times in the Umayyad Mosque. The compass was then transferred to Europe in two stages: the first stage during the Crusades by way of Muslim sailors from the Mediterranean, and the second stage was the era of Ibn Majid in the fifteenth century AD. This was done through the Muslim navigators of South Asia when the Spanish and Italian sailors sought their help.

Conservation Laws

"Allah is the Creator of all things, and He is, over all things, Disposer of affairs. To Him belong the keys of the heavens and the earth."

(Quran 39:62-63)

Certain Quranic verses contain deeper meanings that invite us to contemplate creation's mysteries. They guide us toward recognizing our Creator's infinite knowledge and absolute control over all existence. The "keys" mentioned in this verse may represent the Divine Laws governing universal operation. Every planet, creature, and atom submits to these laws without exception.

"And indeed, it is We who give life and cause death, and We are the Inheritor"

(Quran 15:23)

This verse establishes the Divine Law of Conservation within Allah's absolute authority over life and death. Multiple Quranic passages, including An-Najm (53:44), Ghafir (40:68), and Yunus (10:56), affirm this principle. Only Allah possesses the power to create and destroy, demonstrating His complete sovereignty over existence. There is an assurance to humankind that all earthly sustenance is created and protected by Allah (SWT) which He brings forth in precise quantities as mentioned in this Quranic verse *"There is not a thing but that with Us are its depositories, and We do not send it down except according* to a known [i.e., specified] measure (Quran 15:21). This emphasizes that Allah's actions are not random but are guided by a specific Divine Laws, reflecting His profound wisdom and power. Since He is the one who give life and causes death, Allah (SWT) is therefore the only one who creates and destroys matter, electrical charges, and energy as He wills. Therefore, the changes of mass, charges and energy in the universe follow some Divine Laws.

Conservation of Total Mass

"Let there be no change in this creation of Allah."

(Quran 30:30)

Concerning the conservation of total mass, this Quranic verse indicates clearly that nobody can change what Allah (SWT) has created. Indeed, the law of conservation of total mass states that for any closed system, the total mass of the system must remain constant over time, as the system's mass cannot change, so the quantity can neither be added nor removed, although it may be changed in form. When methane burns with oxygen, it produces carbon dioxide and water. The chemical equation must balance to honor the Divine Law of Conservation of Mass: the total mass of starting materials (methane and oxygen) exactly equals the mass of final products (carbon dioxide and water). This balance reflects Allah's perfect order in creation.

$$CH_4 + 2O_2 \rightarrow CO_2 + 2H_2O \qquad (3)$$

In this topic, the Muslim Scientist Nasir Al-Din al-Tusi (13th Century) stated an early version of the Divine Law of Conservation of Mass. He wrote: "A body of matter cannot disappear completely. It only changes its form, condition, composition, color and other properties and turns into a different complex or elementary matter", which was 500 years ago by Lomonosov and Lavoisier.

"O Children of Adam! wear your beautiful apparel at every time and place of prayer: eat and drink: But waste not by excess, for Allah loveth not the wasters."

(Quran 7:31)

The universe serves as Allah's school for humanity, teaching us through the conservation of mass to use nature wisely and carefully. Modern environmental efforts echo this divine lesson: we must produce, process, and consume natural resources responsibly, recognizing them as sacred trusts from our Creator. However, fourteen centuries ago and based on this Quranic verse, Islam is a guiding light to promote sustainable development in Islamic countries as well as around the world. Indeed, nature should be conserved even during our divine obligations. The Prophet (SAW) exemplified this principle by using minimal water: one mudd (half liter) for ablution and one sa' (two liters) for ritual bathing [Sahih al-Bukhari 201]. His careful use of even basic resources like water provides a timeless model for environmental consciousness and gratitude for Allah's provisions. Using a minimal amount of water wherever possible is encouraged and is a positive approach to our resources. Even so, it involves performing rituals for worship, such as the ablution (wudhu) and obligatory bath (ghusl). We are taught by the Prophet (SAW) to practice moderation and use only what is needed and to avoid wastage.

Conservation of Total Energy

"But you will never find in the way [i.e., established method] of Allah any change, and you will never find in the way of Allāh1 any alteration"

(Quran 35:43)

This verse confirms that Divine Laws remain unchangeable throughout creation. The Divine Law of Conservation of Energy demonstrates this permanence: within the closed system of our universe, total energy remains constant from the moment of creation. While Allah permits energy to transform from one type to another, the total amount never increases or decreases.

"Shake the trunk of the palm-tree towards yourself and fresh and ripe dates shall fall upon you"

(Quran 19:25)

Consider Mary's story (as) in the Holy Quran: she shook the palm tree, causing dates to fall. This simple action reveals the Divine Law of Energy Conservation. High in the tree, dates possess maximum potential energy while remaining motionless. When they fall, this potential energy converts perfectly into kinetic energy (motion). Upon reaching the ground, all potential energy has transformed into kinetic energy. The total energy remains constant throughout this divinely orchestrated process. There is only a change in the form of mechanical energy from potential energy to kinetic energy.

"And We have made (the night) for your sleep as a mean for rest and have made day to seek your provisions."

(Quran 78:9-11)

Just as Allah commands mass conservation, He guides us toward energy conservation through this verse: using minimal energy to accomplish our tasks and avoiding waste. Islamic principles naturally promote energy efficiency: rising early for Fajr, avoiding extravagance, and maintaining moderate sleep patterns all contribute to energy conservation and environmental stewardship. Modern society has disrupted natural rhythms, with people sleeping after midnight and waking around 8-9 AM. This contradicts the divine pattern established in the Quran and Sunnah: sleeping early and rising before dawn for Fajr prayer. This natural cycle aligns with both spiritual obligations and energy conservation. Indeed, the sunlight, which is the source of illumination from dawn to dusk, has been sufficient for millennia and is still sufficient, as The Prophet (SAW) said, "O Allah, bless my nation in their early mornings." [Sunan ibn Majah].

As a final note, it is worth noting that the conservation of total matter and total energy in the universe means that the amount of matter and energy that Allah (SWT) created in the universe will remain constant until the Day of Resurrection. On the other hand, conserving the natural resources (mass and energy) for humanity has a different meaning, and in this case, it means that we are supposed to consume materials and energy as little as possible during our daily activities to protect nature and the future of our children.

Conservation of Total Electrical Charges

"This is Allah's way, already long established in the past. And you will find no change in Allah's way."

(Quran 48:23)

This Divine Law declares that electrical charges cannot be created or destroyed by any created being. According to this verse, Allah established the universe's total electrical charge at creation, and this balance remains fixed. When positive charge appears in one location, an equal amount of negative charge must appear elsewhere, maintaining perfect equilibrium throughout creation.

When you rub a plastic ruler with cloth, the ruler gains negative charge while the cloth gains an equal positive charge. This everyday example reveals profound cosmic significance. Without this Divine Law maintaining electrical balance, galaxies would carry excess charge. Since electromagnetic forces vastly exceed gravitational forces, any electrical imbalance would tear the universe apart, making life impossible.

"Don't you see that the lightning comes and go back in an eye blink"

[Sahih Muslim Vol. 1, Book 1, Hadith 380]

This hadith reveals lightning's true nature: a massive electrical discharge between clouds and earth. Normally, air blocks electrical flow like a barrier. However, when charge separation becomes too great, nature must restore balance. Allah opens a conductive channel through the air, allowing charges to reunite in a brilliant flash we call lightning. This dramatic display demonstrates the Divine Law of Charge Conservation in action.

The hadith describes lightning's two crucial phases: the downward strike toward earth and the upward return to the cloud. This entire process occurs within milliseconds, faster than human eyes can detect. Only modern high-speed cameras capturing thousands of frames per second revealed what the Prophet (SAW) described fourteen centuries ago. This precise knowledge, impossible to observe without advanced technology, affirms the divine source of prophetic wisdom.

Law of Balance

"As for the sky, He raised it ˹high˺ and set the balance

(Meezan)" (Quran 55:7).

Beyond the conservation laws, Allah (SWT) established perfect balance throughout creation, filling nature with order, beauty, and harmony. This verse points to the universe's delicate equilibrium,

51

where ecosystems maintain stable relationships between all living and non-living elements through divine design. This divine balance manifests through species diversity, genetic variety, and sustainable coexistence within ecosystems. When disturbances occur, Allah's design includes self-correcting mechanisms that restore equilibrium. These feedback systems automatically guide disturbed parameters back to their balanced state, maintaining harmony throughout creation. Natural cycles interweave in perfect harmony, each supporting the others in complementary relationships. Among all creation, only humans bear responsibility for maintaining ecological balance, since our choices directly impact these divine systems. All other creatures naturally follow their programmed roles within Allah's established laws.

It should be noted that the Divine Balance in the universe also governs the planetary orbits and other celestial bodies. Finally, at the atomic level, the stability of a covalent bond depends on the balance of attractive and repulsive forces between the electrons and nuclei of the bonding atoms.

First Law of Motion

The laws of motion perfectly illustrate Divine Balance in physics. The first law states: 'An object at rest remains at rest; an object in motion continues moving at constant speed in a straight line, unless acted upon by an unbalanced force.' When all forces acting on an object cancel each other out, perfect balance results in either rest or uniform motion.

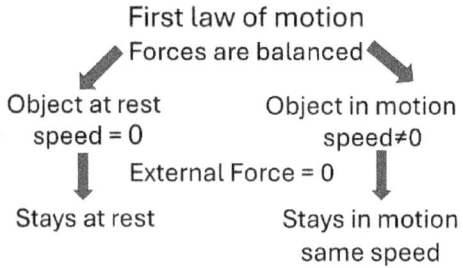

Likewise, a moving object left over with its constant speed state unless it finds any power that shakes it, such as the friction powers. In both situations, and in concordance with this Quranic verse, at rest or motion, there are balanced forces acting on the object.

While Newton receives credit for this law through his Principia, the Muslim scientist Ibn Sina discovered this principle six centuries earlier. In his work 'Insinuations and Notices' (Isharat wa Tanbihat), Ibn Sina wrote: 'You know if the object is left unaffected by external influence, it remains as it is.' This demonstrates how Islamic scholarship anticipated many 'modern' scientific discoveries. In this statement, Ibn Sina asserts that the object remains at rest or in motion with constant speed in a straight line unless external power influences it. That is to say that Ibn Sina was in fact the first to discover the first law of motion.

Second Law of Motion

"That you may not transgress the balance"

(Quran 55:8)"

This verse warns that external forces disrupting the Divine Law of Balance will create disorder and calamity. The second law of motion describes what happens when forces become unbalanced, demonstrating how Allah's perfect equilibrium, once disturbed, produces measurable consequences. When forces become unbalanced, an object's acceleration depends on two factors: the net force applied and the object's mass. Greater force produces greater acceleration, while greater mass reduces acceleration for the same applied force. This mathematical relationship reveals Allah's precise laws governing motion. According to Newton's mathematical formulation of this law: "A body (m) affected by an external force **F** experiences an acceleration **a** related to **F** by:

$$F = m.a \qquad\qquad\qquad (4)$$

The Muslim scientist Hibatullah ibn Malka al-Baghdadi (1087-1164 CE) described this principle centuries before Newton in his work 'Al-Mu'tabar fi'l-Hikma' (The Reliable in Wisdom). He wrote: 'The strongest force produces the fastest motion in the shortest time. Greater force creates greater speed and reduced time. When force remains constant, speed remains constant.' This precisely describes what Newton later mathematically formulated. In chapter fourteen, entitled the Vacuum, he pointed out that "The faster the speed, the stronger the power. The stronger the power that pushes the object, the faster the speed of the object in motion, and the shorter the time spent covering the distance". This is exactly what Newton mathematically formulated.

> "It is Allah Who sends forth winds which then set the clouds in motion, which We drive to some dead land giving a fresh life to earth after it had become dead. Such will be the resurrection of the dead"
>
> (Quran 35:9)

This verse demonstrates the Divine Law of Balance in nature. Without wind as an external force, clouds remain stationary, illustrating the first law of motion. When Allah sends winds to move these clouds according to His will, we witness the second law of motion. Both states reflect perfect divine control over natural forces.

Law of planetary motion

> "He created seven heavens, piled one upon another. In the creation of the All-Merciful, you cannot detect any disparity. Turn your gaze back: do you see any rift? Then turn your gaze back twice more, and your sight will return to you, humbled and flagging"
>
> (Quran 67:3-4)

Celestial bodies maintain perfectly balanced orbits, each following its designated path without collision or chaos. Without this Divine Law, the countless stars and planets would lack harmony in their cosmic dance. Throughout billions of years since Allah (SWT) created the universe, no astronomical records show objects straying from their ordained courses.

In our solar system, two forces create perfect balance: the sun's gravitational pull drawing Earth inward, and Earth's inertia pushing it forward in a straight line. Allah designed these opposing forces to maintain Earth's stable orbit, ensuring consistent seasons and climate for life to flourish.

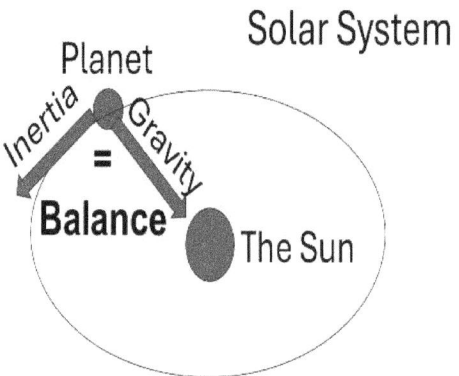

If the Earth were to suddenly stop moving, it would fall directly into the Sun. Therefore, the Divine Law of Balance results in the planet moving in an elliptical orbit around the sun. This is called by Western scientists as Kepler's First Law of Planetary Motion.

"And [He created] the sun, the moon, and the stars, subjected by His command. Unquestionably, He has creation and the command; blessed is Allah, Lord of the worlds."

(Quran 7:54)

Moreover, the orbital radius and angular velocity of the planet in the elliptical orbit will vary. The planet travels faster when closer to the sun, then slower when farther from the Sun. Therefore, the farther the planet is from the sun, the weaker the sun's gravitational pull, and the slower it moves in its orbit. What intelligence guides planets to adjust their speeds at precisely the right moments and locations? This Quranic verse clearly states that Allah created the sun, moon, and stars, governing their movements through His direct command. Western science labels this divine orchestration as 'Kepler's Second Law,' yet the true Commander remains Allah.

Muslims have been interested in what happens in the sky since the Umayyad era, based on the Quranic guidance that calls for contemplation of the creation of the heavens and the earth. The motivation was originally based on faith and religion, as knowledge of the movements of the stars was linked to determining the times of daily prayers. And by calculating the months and years for the obligatory duties of zakat, fasting, the rites of Hajj, and the rituals of the holidays, then this religious motive was mixed with the scientific passion for interpreting cosmic scientific phenomena such as solar and lunar eclipses, and determining the diameters and distances of the planets, celestial bodies, the sun, and the moon. In order to achieve all of this,

Muslims had to establish specialized locations to monitor the movement of planets and celestial bodies in the sky, which they called observatories. Astrono-mical tables were compiled, including the Toledo Tables, which were used by Copernicus, Tycho Brahe, and Kepler. The Toledo Tables are astronomical tables used to predict the movements of the sun, moon, and planets relative to the fixed stars. They were completed around the year 1080 by a group of Arab astronomers in the city of Toledo. In modern astronomy, tables of the movements of astronomical bodies are called the astronomical calendar.

The Law of balance in Muslim societies

"O my people! Give full measure and weigh with balance (Meezan). Do not defraud people of their property, nor go about spreading corruption in the land"

(Quran 11:85)

In Muslim societies, the Arabic word 'Meezan' refers to scales used for weighing goods in trade. Islamic scholarship elevated this practical tool into a powerful symbol of justice and moral conduct. The Quran and Sunnah repeatedly emphasize fair weighing practices, extending this principle from marketplace transactions to all human interactions. Balance serves as Islam's central principle for harmonizing spiritual, social, and material life. Muslims must avoid extremes in work, family obligations, social relationships, and religious duties. When properly applied, this principle creates societies built on justice, compassion, and moderation, fostering equity and fairness for all members.

Mecca served as both spiritual center and a commercial hub before and after Islam's revelation. Many of the Prophet's Companions (SAW) were successful merchants, including Uthman, Abd al-Rahman ibn Awf, and Zubayr ibn al-Awwam. Their business practices demonstrated how Islamic principles of balance and justice could flourish in trade. The study of their approaches in businesses shall enlighten us with the recipes of success in business development based on the two fundamental principles of Islam: Al-Adl (justice) and Al-Ihsan (improvement). These principles were recorded explicitly in several treatises on the balance, such as the introduction to Kitab Meezan al-Hikma (the book of the balance of wisdom) by al-Khazini, where the balance is qualified as "the tongue of justice.

"That you do not transgress within the balance"

(Quran 55: 8)

This verse finds urgent relevance in our environmental crisis. Daily evidence reveals how excessive consumption pushes Earth toward ecological collapse. Our massive carbon emissions from burning fossil fuels disrupt the atmospheric balance Allah (SWT) established. This transgression of divine limits manifests in climate change and environmental destruction. This disruption traps excess heat in our atmosphere, causing global warming and triggering natural disasters. When we transgress Allah's established balance, the environment struggles to restore equilibrium. The result threatens the beauty and blessings Allah placed in each season, diminishing the natural signs that point us toward our Creator.

Divine Laws of Charity

"We will show them Our signs in the universe and in their own selves, until it becomes manifest to them that this (the Quran) is the truth."

(Quran; 41:53)

Beyond the Divine Law of Balance, Allah (SWT) established Divine Laws of Charity governing the universe. Charity represents the transfer of resources from areas of abundance to areas of need. How does this manifest in creation? The Fashioner (SWT) designed Earth as a sphere where the sun heats equatorial regions more intensely than polar areas, creating energy-rich and energy-poor zones across our planet. This uneven solar heating creates energy imbalances across Earth's surface. How does nature restore divine equilibrium? Allah's wisdom operates through Two Divine Laws of Charity that govern these energy transfers. We can observe these laws most clearly in the water cycle that sustains all life.

First Divine Law of Charity

"As for the sky, He raised it ˈhighˈ, and set the balance"

(Quran 55:7

The Sustainer and Most Wise (SWT) restores natural balance by directing matter and energy to flow from areas of high concentration to areas of low concentration. While scientific textbooks call this the second law of thermodynamics, we recognize it as Allah's First Divine Law of Charity governing all natural flows.

This law governs all natural transfers: heat moves from hot to cold, fluids flow from high to low pressures, and objects fall from higher to lower elevations.

Every natural flow in creation follows this divine principle of charitable transfer from abundance to need:

$$E_{High} \ (concentrated) \ \rightarrow \ E_{low} \ (diluted) \qquad (5)$$

"The seven heavens and the Earth and all that is therein, glorify Him and there is not a thing but glorifies His Praise. But you understand not their glorification"

(Quran; 17.44)

This verse reveals profound truth: viewing energy as 'wealth,' the entire universe glorifies Allah (SWT) through constant acts of charity. Every natural flow demonstrates cosmic generosity as energy-rich regions share their abundance with energy-poor areas, reflecting the divine character of giving.

Consequently, Equation (6) is simply the 1st Divine Law of Charity imposed by Allah (SWT) on the universe and can be rewritten as:

$$Rich \ (in \ energy) \rightarrow Poor \ (in \ energy) \qquad (6)$$

Consider a simple battery: the anode, rich in electrons, naturally gives up electrons to the cathode, which has fewer electrons. This everyday device demonstrates the First Divine Law of Charity, where abundance flows toward need, powering our daily lives through Allah's established principles.

In this case, the 1ˢᵗ Divine Law of Charity is known in scientific textbooks as the Electromotive force (Emf), defined as the characteristic of any "energy source" capable of driving electrons inside an electrical circuit.

> *"And there is not a thing but that with Us are its depositories, and We do not send it down except according to a known measure."*

(Quran; 15:21)

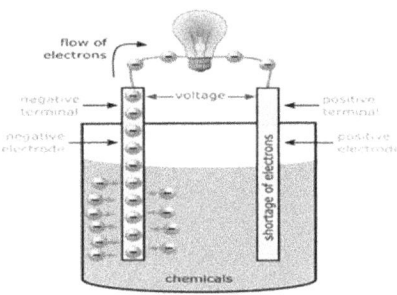

Second Divine Law of Charity

This verse reveals that Allah, the All-Authoritative, determines the precise measure of everything transported throughout the universe.

Natural flows not only move from energy-rich to energy-poor regions, but their exact quantity and timing follow a second divine decree that governs all movement in creation. The Quranic verse *"And We sent down from the sky water in due measure"*(Quran 23:18) confirms that rainfall amounts and timing are divinely predetermined. This spiritual truth aligns with scientific observation: all natural flows follow a mathematical relationship where flow rate depends on the driving force and resistance encountered, expressed in this general transport equation:

$$Flow \propto \frac{Driving\ Force}{Resistance} \qquad\qquad (7)$$

In order to link this general equation of transport phenomena to the above Quranic verse, the difference in energy between a region in Earth having high energy (E_{High}) and a region having lower energy (E_{low}) is considered as the "driving force" of any natural flow and, the fluid or solid between these two regions presents a resistance "R" to the flow under consideration. Based on Equation (7), the flow of matter or energy transported in nature could be qualitatively represented by:

$$Flow\ \left(\frac{Amount\ of\ matter\ or\ energy}{time}\right) \propto \frac{(E_{Rich} - E_{Poorer})}{R} \qquad (8)$$

In concordance with the above Quranic verse, Equation (8) is therefore the 2nd Divine Law of Charity that determines the amount of transported matter or energy predetermined by Allah (SWT). Consider heat conduction in metal as a spiritual lesson: thermal energy flows like charity from the "wealthy" hot region (T_2) to the "needy" cold region (T_1). This everyday phenomenon demonstrates how Allah embedded the principle of giving into the very fabric of matter itself.

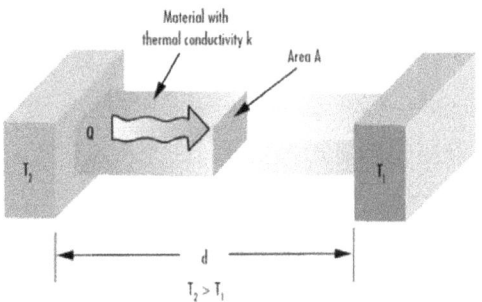

Furthermore, to use Equation (8), the **"gradient of energy"** ($E_{Rich} - E_{poorer}$) is represented by the difference in temperature ($T_2 - T_1$) between the two parts of the material. Considering the thermal conductivity (conductance) of the material (**k**), its inverse (**1/k**) is therefore the resistance to the heat flow (Q). Therefore, based on Equation (8), the amount of **richness** (Q) given as charity can be qualitatively expressed by Equation (9):

$$Flow\ of\ Charity\ \left(\frac{Q}{t}\right) \propto \frac{(T_2 - T_1)}{\left(\frac{1}{k}\right)} \qquad (9)$$

Nature teaches us a profound lesson: Allah requires every abundant entity to share a predetermined portion with those in need, creating balance and harmony throughout creation. This divine law of charitable distribution operates from atomic interactions to cosmic movements. Fourier's law of heat conduction, familiar to engineers worldwide, actually expresses the Second Divine Law of Charity in mathematical form. What science calls a physical law, we recognize as Allah's charitable principle governing thermal energy distribution:

$$Flow\ of\ Charity\ \left(\frac{Q}{t}\right) = \frac{(t_2 - t_1)}{\frac{1}{k}} \qquad (10)$$

This same Divine Law appears across all scientific disciplines: as Fick's law governing matter diffusion in chemical engineering, and as Ohm's law controlling electron flow in electrical engineering. Every natural flow throughout creation obeys these two Divine Laws of Charity that Allah (SWT) embedded in the universe's foundation.

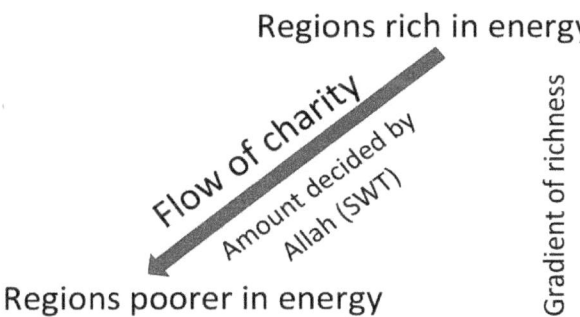

Signs of charity & the season of spring in nature

> *"And in the waters which Allah sends down from the sky, giving life thereby to the Earth after it had, been lifeless, and causing all manner of living creatures to multiply thereon: and in the change of the winds, and the clouds that run their appointed courses between sky and Earth: [in all this] there are Signs indeed for people who use their reason"*

> (Quran 2:164)

This verse beautifully describes the water cycle, one of Allah's most remarkable designs. The Creator endowed water with unique properties enabling continuous regeneration through evaporation from oceans and condensation in clouds. Each stage of this cycle demonstrates how Allah made water an eternally renewable source sustaining all life on Earth.

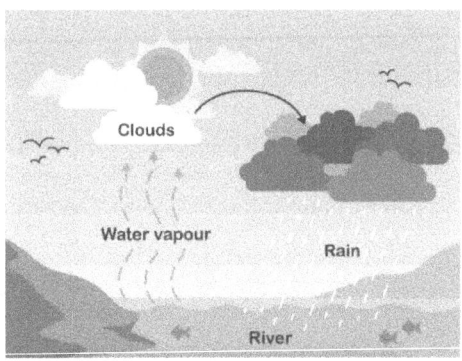

Through the water cycle, we witness Allah's Beautiful Names in action as natural flows demonstrate the Two Divine Laws of Charity across the changing seasons. Each season reveals different aspects of divine charity sustaining life on Earth.

Evaporation of water using solar radiation

"And We have made (therein) a shining lamp (sun)"

(Quran; 78:13)

During summer's warmth, while people bask in sunshine, the sun's intense energy quietly initiates water evaporation from vast oceans. This invisible yet vital process reflects Allah's Beautiful Name 'Al-

Latif (The Subtle One), whose work often remains hidden from our immediate perception yet sustains all life. In this opening act of the water cycle, the First Divine Law of Charity governs the process. Water vapor pressure reaches its maximum at sea level and gradually decreases toward the sky, creating the driving force for evaporation. This pressure difference demonstrates how abundance naturally flows toward areas of lesser concentration. Regarding the 2nd Divine Law of Charity, the gradient of richness ($P_{w, sea} - P_{w, sky}$) between sea level and the sky is considered as the "driving force" of the evaporation process of water. Moreover, using the convective (conductance) mass transfer coefficient (k_{air}) of water in the atmospheric air, the flow of evaporation of water is regulated by the resistance ($1/k_{air}$). As mentioned in this Quranic verse, the sun is the source of energy for the water cycle and the flow of water evaporated is qualitatively expressed by the equation:

$$Flow\ of\ evaporation\ (WE) \propto \frac{(P_{w,sea} - P_{w,sky})}{\left(\frac{1}{k_{air}}\right)}\ \left(\frac{Driving\ force}{Resitance}\right)\quad (11)$$

To calculate the flow (WE), scientists in hydrometeorology use the Penman equation. This equation is based on measurements of the mean of sea temperature, wind speed, air pressure, and solar radiation.

Transportation of vapor using wind power

"And it is Allah Who sends the winds, so they can raise up the clouds, and We drive them to a dead land"

(Quran; 35:9)

As autumn arrives and children return to school, seasonal winds begin their vital work of transporting moisture-laden clouds from oceans to land. These powerful winds reflect Allah's Beautiful Name 'Al-Qadeer' (The All-Powerful), demonstrating how He moves vast quantities of water across continents to nourish distant lands. As mentioned in this Quranic verse, this second stage of the water cycle will obey the 1st Divine Law of Charity when air over oceans will have higher values of atmospheric pressure (P_{High}) than the atmospheric pressure (P_{low}) of air over land. During this period of time and to utilize the 2nd Divine Law of Charity, the gradient of richness (P_{High}- P_{low}) is taken as the driving force of the transportation process of clouds by the power of winds. The flow of water in the clouds is regulated by the friction (R_{air}) caused by atmospheric air. Therefore, similar to the evaporation process, the flow of transported of water by the winds (WT) could be qualitatively expressed by the equation:

$$Flow\ of\ transportation\ (WT) \propto \frac{(P_{High}-P_{low})}{R_{air}}\ (\frac{Driving\ force}{Resistance})\ \ (12)$$

The flow (WT) transported is usually quantified using the advection equation, and the two most important parameters that affect the process are the strength and the angle of the wind.

Precipitation using Earth's gravity

"He sends down water (rain) from the sky, and therewith revives the Earth after its death"

(Quran; 30:24)

As winter's chill sends people reaching for warm coats and darkens the clouds overhead, rain and snow begin to fall. This final stage beautifully demonstrates the First Divine Law of Charity: water suspended high in clouds possesses maximum potential energy, which it generously releases as it descends to Earth, delivering life-giving moisture where it's needed most. The Second Divine Law of Charity operates through gravity's pull, creating the driving force for precipitation. Here we witness Allah's mercy as 'Ar-Rahman' (The Bestower of Mercy): He designed air resistance to slow falling raindrops. Without this divine protection, rain would plummet like bullets, destroying crops and endangering all life on Earth. Therefore, the precipitation of water (rain or snow) could be qualitatively described by the equation:

$$Precipitation \ (WF) \propto \frac{(PE_{High} - PE_{low})}{R_{air}} \left(\frac{Driving \ force}{Resistance} \right) \qquad (13)$$

This amount (WF) is usually calculated by the "intensity of rainfall," which indicates the amount of rain that falls over time, and it is measured in millimeters per hour (mm/h).

The Season of Spring

After summer's evaporation, autumn's transportation, and winter's precipitation, spring arrives like nature's celebration. Through His Beautiful Names 'Al-Kareem' (The Most Generous) and 'Ar-Razzaq' (The Sustainer), Allah brings forth abundance and renewal. Birds burst into song, flowers paint the earth in brilliant colors, and life awakens from winter's rest. Just as Allah brings the spiritually dead to life through guidance, He resurrects the earth through spring's touch. As this heavenly season reaches its peak, the eternal cycle of divine charity begins anew, demonstrating Allah's endless generosity in sustaining all creation.

Transportation- Autumn

Precipitation Cyclic flow Evaporation
Winter   of charity   Summer

Reward of Spring

Muslim scientists of the Golden Age made pioneering contributions to understanding the water cycle through careful observation of atmospheric phenomena. Ibn Duraid al-Azdi, who flourished in the late 9th and early 10th centuries, authored the groundbreaking work 'Description of Rain and Clouds,' providing the first systematic scientific study of these processes. The first of two editions was by the English Orientalist William Right (1830–1889), the second by Ezidden Al-Tanokhi (Damascus 1963). This remarkable work's 27 chapters provide humanity's first scientific descriptions of rain and clouds. Ibn Duraid systematically covered weather forecasting, cloud formation and movement, precipitation types, and their effects on soil and groundwater. His observations laid the foundation for modern meteorology centuries before European developments. The book also describes cloud topography. It also observes clouds as they lie upon each other, such as Al-Rabab (clouds that connect with others), and their form regarding the Earth's surface and topographic relief. It also describes their shades and colors. His work also divides lightning, according to the intensity of its light: Al-hafo, the weakest form, Al-wamed, which resembles a little smile, and Al-wallaf, which strikes twice.

Divine Law of Charity in Muslim societies

"Have you not seen that Allah has subjected to your service all that is in the heavens and on the earth and has abundantly bestowed upon you all His bounties, both visible and invisible? Yet some persons dispute regarding Allah without having any knowledge or guidance or any illuminating Book"

(Quran 31:20)

Since the universe is a divine school, the same way Allah (SWT) imposed His Divine Laws of Charity on the universe, He also orders charity for Muslims in the Holy Quran and Sunnah. In addition, the Beautiful Names of Allah (SWT) mentioned in the Holy Quran and the Prophetic Sunnah also have signs in the universe. For example, in this Quranic verse, Allah (SWT) describes Himself as "Generous" and, therefore, commanded us also to be generous as well.

This verse showcases Allah's boundless generosity by cataloging His gifts to humanity: vast skies, fertile lands, life-sustaining oceans, majestic mountains, flowing rivers, the radiant sun, gentle moon, and countless galaxies beyond our sight. Every breath we take, every bite we eat, every moment of beauty we witness flows from His inexhaustible generosity to all living beings. His provision is endless, including all material things, like money, food, water, air, shelter, and protection. As He meets our physiological needs, He also takes care of our psychological needs. For example, He gives us love through the love of our parents.

"You will never attain piety until you spend out of what you hold dear, and whatever you may spend of anything, Allah indeed knows it"

(Quran; 3: 92)

Allah's generosity extends to our very nature: He created us with sound Fitrah (innate goodness), embedding kindness, compassion, and noble qualities into our souls. This divine compass naturally guides us toward charitable acts that bring genuine happiness and prepare us for eternal bliss in Paradise. Children instinctively demonstrate this goodness before worldly influences cloud their pure hearts. As adults, we are also ordered to share part of the wealth He provided to us with the less fortunate to purify our souls. In this topic, Allah (SWT) describes the pious as those who share with the others everything, He provided them as He says, *"This is the Book! There is no doubt about it—a guide for the pious who believe in the unseen, establish prayer, and spend out of what We have provided for them" (Quarn 2:2-3)*. The most important thing is that pleasing Allah (SWT) should be the sole reason for helping people, animals, and plants during our social and professional activities.

> *"Who are niggardly and bid others to be niggardly and conceal the bounty which Allah has bestowed upon them. We have kept in readiness a humiliating chastisement for such deniers (of Allah's bounty"*
>
> (Quran 4:37)

Charity forms faith's backbone, as reflected in the Arabic word 'sadaqah,' derived from 'tasdeeq' (truthfulness). Our charitable acts serve as visible proof of inner belief, transforming abstract faith into concrete action. While the Quran and Sunnah extensively praise generosity and spending for Allah's sake, they equally warn against the spiritual poison of miserliness and hoarding. This verse delivers a stark warning: those who hoard Allah's blessings while others suffer in need are counted among the disbelievers. By refusing to share what Allah has entrusted to them, misers position themselves as enemies of the Most High, rejecting the very purpose for which wealth was given.

Laws of Creation and Decay

> *"Indeed, We established him upon the earth, and We gave him to everything a way. So, he followed a way"*
>
> (Quran 18:84-85)

The story of Dhul-Qarnain reveals how Allah empowered this righteous king by providing him with the means to achieve his goals.

Allah gave him pathways to everything he needed, and he followed these divinely appointed routes. This narrative illustrates how Allah established cause-and-effect relationships throughout creation, embedding Divine Laws that govern the scientific connections between actions and outcomes. At the same time, Allah designed our minds to recognize patterns and accept His wisdom through observable cause and effect. When illness strikes and medicine brings healing, we consider this natural. Yet every cure depends on permission from Allah, the Ultimate Healer. He could heal through prayer alone, through acts of charity, or through any means He chooses, reminding us that all healing flows from His grace. Allah demonstrates His absolute sovereignty through the verse: *"Honorable Owner of the Throne, Doer of whatever He wills "*(Quran 85:15-16). Sometimes natural causes produce no effect, as when healthy couples remain childless despite medical intervention. Other times, effects occur without natural causes, as in the miraculous birth of Jesus (as) without a father, reminding us that Allah transcends the very laws He established.

Creation in Pairs

"And We created pairs of all things so perhaps you would be mindful"

(Quran 51:49)

This verse reveals the Divine Law of Pairs governing all creation. Beyond the Laws of Balance and Charity, Allah established that natural forces operate in complementary pairs. Science recognizes these as action and reaction forces, but we understand them as reflections of Allah's wisdom in creating everything with its perfect counterpart.

When you push against an object, it pushes back with equal force in the opposite direction. This everyday experience demonstrates paired forces working in perfect equilibrium. Ibn Bajjah (1085-1138) formulated this principle centuries before Newton, proposing that every force produces a corresponding reaction force. Though he didn't specify their equality, his insight anticipated what European science would later call

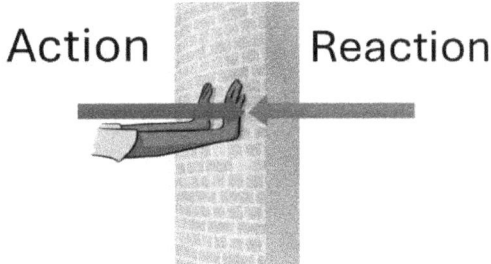

"But when they reached the point where the two rivers meet, they forgot their fish, and it took its way into the sea, as if through a tunnel"

(Quran 18:61)

Nature showcases action-reaction pairs throughout creation. Swimming fish demonstrate this principle beautifully: they generate thrust by pushing water backward, while water pushes them forward with equal force. Simultaneously, their weight pulls downward while buoyancy pushes upward, creating a perfect equilibrium that allows them to navigate through water with divine precision.

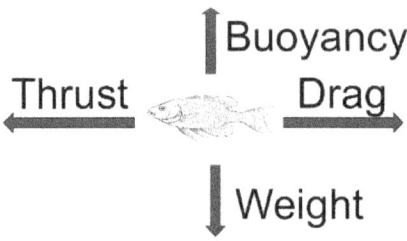

When fish swim at a steady speed, thrust and drag forces equilibrate perfectly. To accelerate, they must generate greater thrust to overcome water resistance. Meanwhile, the equilibrium between their weight and the water's buoyant force allows them to maintain their chosen depth effortlessly. What scientists call Archimedes' principle, we recognize as Allah's Divine Law of Pairs governing aquatic life.

> *"Do they not see the birds made to fly through the air in the sky? Nothing holds them up except Allah. There truly are signs in this for those who believe"*
>
> (Qur'an 16:79)

Birds soaring through the heavens demonstrate the same Divine Law of Pairs. Four forces govern their flight: lift opposes weight, while thrust overcomes drag. These paired forces work in perfect harmony through Allah's inspiration, allowing birds to master aerodynamic principles without any engineering training. In this case, The Divine

Law of Pairs is also known in scientific textbooks as Newton's third law of motion.

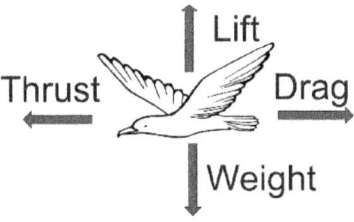

This verse reveals that birds remain airborne through the Divine Law of Pairs. Their mastery of aerodynamics continues to amaze scientists who study their effortless flight. For steady, level flight, birds generate lift to counter gravity and thrust to overcome drag. When these forces equilibrate perfectly, birds glide with the grace Allah embedded in their design. When birds accelerate, they increase thrust beyond drag force, demonstrating precise control over aerodynamic principles. Watching these magnificent creatures soar effortlessly through Allah's vast sky naturally draws our hearts to glorify their Creator. Their innate mastery of flight mechanics continues to humble human engineers and inspire new technologies.

> "It is He Who created the night and the day, and the sun and the moon. Each of them is floating in its orbit".
>
> (Quran 21:33)

This verse reveals additional evidence of the Divine Law of Pairs operating through creation's fundamental rhythms. Day and night form one pair, while sun and moon constitute another. Allah created these complementary opposites with perfect planning and precise balance, enabling us to measure time, track seasons, and organize our lives according to celestial patterns. Life on Earth depends entirely on the sun and moon's precisely calibrated distances from our planet. Allah positioned these celestial bodies with mathematical perfection: any random increase or decrease in their distances would obliterate all life. This divine precision in cosmic architecture demonstrates Allah's meticulous planning for sustaining His creation.

Decay Process

> *"All that is on it (- the earth) is subject to decay and doomed to pass away."*
>
> (Quran 55:26)

Science describes natural decay through the second law of thermodynamics, focusing on entropy as a measure of disorder. What scientists call 'the law of entropy' reveals that all systems naturally progress from organized, ordered states toward increasing disorder and dispersion. This universal tendency toward decay operates throughout Allah's creation. The Divine Law of Decay governs the universe's inevitable progression toward greater disorder and disorganization. This principle, universally accepted by scientists as fundamental to understanding natural processes, reveals Allah's appointed end for the current creation, pointing toward the eventual resurrection and renewal of all things. Darwin's evolutionary mechanism directly contradicts the

Divine Law of Decay. Evolution claims that random, lifeless atoms and molecules spontaneously organized themselves into increasingly complex structures like proteins, DNA, and RNA, eventually producing millions of sophisticated living species. This proposed progression from disorder to order violates the fundamental principle of entropy. Evolution proposes that increasingly organized and complex structures emerge naturally from disorder, contradicting the Divine Law of Decay. This Quranic verse points to the universe's ultimate fate: matter and energy will continue dispersing until maximum disorder is reached and all processes cease. Scientists call this endpoint the 'heat death of the universe,' marking the conclusion of the current creation before Allah's promised renewal.

"And when the stars fall, dispersing"

(Quran 81:2)

This verse may allude to black holes, regions where gravity becomes so intense that even light cannot escape. These cosmic phenomena form when massive stars collapse at the end of their lives, compressing enormous amounts of matter into incredibly small spaces. The resulting gravitational field becomes so powerful that it warps space and time itself. Recent theoretical physics suggests that cosmic transformation could spread as an expanding sphere moving at the speed of light. This process might fundamentally alter the universe's structure, making particles heavier and gravitational forces stronger than the forces that currently hold atoms together. Such a transformation would cause matter to collapse at the atomic level, reshaping creation in ways only Allah fully comprehends.

Creation of Pairs and Decay for humankind

Before exploring how the laws of creation and decay apply to humanity, we should recognize that Allah's Beautiful Names sometimes appear to express opposite qualities, as revealed in these verses:

"He is the First and the Last, and the Manifest and the Hidden, and He has knowledge of everything"

(Quran 57:3)

"Say: 'O Allah, Lord of all dominion! You give dominion to whom You will, and take away dominion from whom You will, and You exalt whom You will, and abase whom You will. In Your Hand is all good. Surely You are All-Powerful"

(Quran 3:26)

The second verse clarifies this apparent paradox: "In Your hand is all good" reveals that even seemingly opposite divine qualities serve beneficial purposes for humanity and creation. Allah's justice and mercy, His giving and withholding, all work together for ultimate good according to His perfect wisdom. "And We created pairs of all things so perhaps you would be mindful."

(Quran 51:49)

This verse reveals Allah's design of universal pairs: male and female, night and day, heat and cold in the physical realm, alongside truth and falsehood, faith and disbelief, guidance and misguidance in the spiritual realm. This pairing demonstrates Allah's perfect power to create any reality He wills, including complementary opposites that together form complete systems.

> *"Whoever will come to Allah with a good deed shall have ten times as much, and whoever will come to Allah with an evil deed, shall be requited with no more than the like of it. They shall not be wronged"*
>
> (Quran 6:160)

This magnificent verse reveals Allah's special treatment of humanity: He multiplies rewards for good deeds beyond the universal law of equal action and reaction that governs the physical world. For evil deeds, He applies justice equally or offers forgiveness, demonstrating mercy that transcends the mechanical laws governing the rest of creation. As Allah's vicegerents on Earth, we are commanded to apply proportional justice in human affairs, responding to others as they treat us. The verse *"Fight in the way of Allah those who fight you but do not transgress. Indeed, Allah does not like transgressors"* (Quran 2:190) establishes this principle. Allah forbids us from exceeding proper bounds in retaliation, maintaining justice without becoming oppressors ourselves. "Following Allah's example as 'Al-Ghafur' (The Forgiver), we are encouraged to choose the higher path of forgiveness and responding to evil with good. The Quran teaches: "And not equal are the good deed and the bad. Repel evil by that which is better; and thereupon the one whom between you and him is enmity will become as though he was a devoted friend" (Quran 41:34). This divine strategy transforms enemies into allies through the power of goodness.

"Saying, "My Lord! Surely my bones have become brittle, and grey hair has spread across my head"

(Quran 19:4)

This verse poignantly describes human aging: our bodies gradually weaken, bones become fragile, and hair turns grey as signs of the Divine Law of Decay operating within us. Since bones provide our structural foundation, keeping us upright and mobile, their weakening affects our entire physical capacity, reminding us of our temporary nature in this world.

"There is no god but He, everything is perishable but He; His is the judgment, and to Him you shall be brought back"

(Quran 28:88)

Concerning human resurrection on Judgment Day, authentic prophetic hadiths describe the tailbone (coccyx) as both the origin of fetal development and the indestructible seed of resurrection. This small bone reportedly survives bodily decomposition, serving as the foundation from which Allah will reconstruct our bodies on the Day of Judgment. When Allah wills resurrection, He sends rain from heaven, causing each person to grow from their preserved tailbone like a plant sprouting from its seed. Abu Hurairah (may Allah be pleased with him) narrated that the Messenger of Allah (peace and blessings be upon him) said:

"The earth consumes every part of the son of Adam except the tailbone, from which he was created and from which he will be resurrected"

[Abu Dawud, Al-Nasa'i, Ahmad, Ibn Majah, Ibn Hibban, Malik].

Tawhidic Paradigm

"See you not that whoever is in the heavens and whoever is on the earth, and the sun, and the moon, and the stars, and the mountains, and the trees, and living creatures, beasts, and many of mankind, prostrate themselves to Allah"

(Quran; 22:18)

We conclude this exploration of divine laws with the Tawhidic Paradigm - the unifying principle revealing Allah's Oneness through all creation. Allah established the universe under Divine Forces and Laws, maintaining perfect natural balance. The harmony in celestial movements, plant growth, ocean currents, mountain stability, animal behavior, day-night cycles, and birth processes testifies to these divine principles. Contemplating creation forms the cornerstone of Islamic spirituality, leading us to recognize Allah's absolute unity governing all existence. In fact, in this Quranic verse, Allah (SWT) commands us to reflect on His creation. Why? Because the first realization is undoubtedly Tawhid (monotheism).

"And they reflect on the creation of the heavens and the Earth, 'and pray Our Lord! You have not created 'all' this without purpose. Glory be to You! Protect us from the torment of the Fire.

(Quran 3:191).

The greatest and most evident signs of Allah (SWT) in the universe are the sun, the moon, and the alternation of day and night. They are always present in front of every human being. Moreover, the connection between the universe and the Holy Quran can also be understood through the fact that some of Allah (SWT)'s creations are the names of some of the chapters of the Holy Quran, such as the sheep, the bee, the ant, the dawn, the sun, the night, mankind, the earthquake, and others. In fact, there are more than a thousand Quranic verses related to the universe, and therefore, knowledge in Islam includes not only the religious knowledge (Ayat from the Holy Quran) but also the worldly knowledge (Ayat from the universe).

"If, after the knowledge you have received, you follow their desires, you will certainly be counted among the transgressors"

(Quran 2:145)

In conclusion, the concept of science in Islam is the concept of the Tawhidic Paradigm, namely the belief in Allah (SWT) alone in all aspects of His creation and commands in the universe. In fact, seeking knowledge in the universe without Tawheed will cause humans to forget themselves and neglect their divine obligations and goals in life. On the other hand, a Muslim who does not seek knowledge in the universe is not fully satisfying the divine duty and cannot build a strong Ummah because knowledge should be learned as Allah (SWT) says

"And that man attains only what he strives for

(Quran 53:39)

"They are not but [mere] names you have named them – you and your forefathers – for which Allah has sent down no authority. They follow not except assumption and what [their] souls desire, and there has already come to them from their Lord guidance"

(Quran 53:23)

Before starting the third and last part of the book related to natural sciences in Islam, it is worth mentioning that the divine forces and divine laws are given other names in scientific textbooks based on atheism. Indeed, in these textbooks, the divine force of gravity is attributed to the scientists who discovered this divine law, namely, Isaac Newton and Johannes Kepler. The divine force of magnetism is attributed to Michael Faraday, the divine law of conservation of mass is attributed to Antoine Lavoisier, and the divine law of conservation of energy is part of the first law of thermodynamics. The law of conservation of electrical charges is attributed to William Watson, the divine law of balance is called Newton's first and second laws of motion or Kepler's first and second laws, and the first divine law of charity is attributed to the second law of thermodynamics, and the second law of charity is related to the science of transport phenomena. Finally, the divine law of creation in pairs is related to the third Newton's law of motion and Archimede's principle, while the divine law of decay is related to the entropy of the second law of thermodynamics.

Islam & Science

"Indeed, Allah conferred a great favor on the believers when He sent among them a Messenger from among themselves, reciting to them His verses (the Quran) and purifying them and instructing them the Book (Quran) and wisdom (Sunnah), while before that they had been in manifest error."

(Quran; 3:164)

Islamic education emerged from the profound unity between religious instruction and worldly knowledge. From its inception, Islam elevated learning as both a spiritual obligation and a practical necessity, creating a rich intellectual tradition spanning centuries. What distinguishes Islamic education is the Quran's all-encompassing influence, integrating spiritual and empirical knowledge into a unified worldview. Since the Quran serves as Allah's direct communication to humanity, early Muslims eagerly pursued literacy to access its full blessings, making reading and writing foundational skills for spiritual and intellectual development.

"They replied: Glory be to You! We have no knowledge except what You have taught us. You are truly the All-Knowing, All-Wise."

(Quran 2:32)

Allah remains the ultimate source of all knowledge and sciences. Just as He taught Adam the names of all things, establishing the foundation of human learning, Allah's knowledge encompasses all existence without beginning or end, free from the trial and error that characterizes human discovery. Yet Allah commands us to seek knowledge through observation and reflection on His creation, reminding us: "But above those ranking in knowledge is the One All-Knowing"

(Quran 12:76).

This verse keeps human achievement in proper perspective while encouraging scientific pursuit. Science from Allah (SWT) is in fact the Life and Light that helps believers see the Truth, as Allah (SWT) says, "And is one who was dead, and We gave him life and made for him light by which to walk among the people like one who is in darkness, never to emerge therefrom? (Quran 6:122). To reinforce this Quranic verse, The Prophet (SAW) said:

"If anyone pursues a path in knowledge, Allah (SWT) will thereby make easy for him a path to the Paradise; and he who is made slow by his actions will not be sped by his genealogy" [Kitab Al-Ilm: Book 19, Number 3636:]. The Prophet (SAW) also said "Seeking knowledge is an obligation for every Muslim man and woman"

[Sunan Ibn Mājah 224].

Islamic Approach to Science

"Behold! In the creation of the heavens and the Earth, In the disparity of night and day, In the ship which runs upon the sea for the profit of mankind, In the water which God sent down from the sky thereby reviving the Earth after its death, In the beasts of all kinds He scatters therein, In the change of the winds and the subjected clouds between the sky and Earth, Here are Signs for people who are wise."

(Quran 2:164)

Despite being revealed in 7th-century Arabia, the Quran contains scientific insights that align remarkably with modern discoveries unknown to that era's people. This convergence between Quranic descriptions and contemporary science demonstrates the text's divine origin. Consider this verse describing natural phenomena:

"He is the One who spread out the Earth and set therein mountains standing firm and rivers. For every fruit He placed two of a pair. He covers the day with the night. Verily in this there are Signs for people who reflect"

(Quran 13:3).

Such descriptions invite scientific exploration while affirming divine authorship. For example, modern scientific discoveries, such as those in genetics, cell life, and quantum physics, were hardly imaginable in the era of the Prophet (SAW). Yet, the Holy Quran amazingly refers to these discoveries. The Holy Quran contains also evidence on the Theory of Relativity, Big Bang Theory, Genetics, Black Holes, and more. Evidently, the Words (Quran) of the Creator (SWT) and science are not isolated from each other.

> *"Produce your proof if you are truthful."*
>
> (Quran 2:111).

Based on this Quranic verse, Allah (SWT) commands us to always bring the proof when seeking scientific knowledge. In this perspective, the empiricism (The practice of basing ideas and theories on testing and experience) in modern natural and social sciences is a known reality of our epistemology. Indeed, Allah (SWT) announces this fact clearly in the following Quranic verse *"And pursue not that of which you have no knowledge; for every act of hearing, or of seeing or of (feeling in) the heart will be inquired into (on the Day of Reckoning)" (Quran 17:36).* In other words, our conclusion should not be based on superstitions but rather on scientific analysis to come up with results and final decisions in all facets of our life.

> *"This is because Allah is the Truth, and that which they call upon besides Him is the falsehood, and that Allah is the High, the Great."*
>
> (Quran 31:30)

Allah calls Muslim scientists to study the universe and discover the divine principles governing celestial and terrestrial phenomena.

Recognizing Allah's absolute Power, Wisdom, and Knowledge through scientific investigation humbles researchers while inspiring deeper study of the Quran and Sunnah. This pursuit reveals divine laws embedded throughout creation, transforming scientific research from mere curiosity into an act of worship and spiritual discovery. In this regard, many Quranic verses refer to creations as divine signs, such as:

"Do they not look at the Camels, how they are made? And in the Sky, how is it raised high? And at Mountains, how are they fixed? And on the Earth, how is it spread out?"

(Quran 88:17-20)

"The Sun and the Moon follow courses (exactly) computed."

(Quran 55:5)

"He it is who gave the sun radiance and the moon light and determined the stages that you may learn the calculation of years and the reckoning of time. Allah has created all this with a rightful purpose. He explains His signs for the people who know"

(Quran 10:5)

According to these Quranic verses, Muslim scientists are expected to observe natural phenomena and study their Divine Commandments and organizations within the framework of The Holy Quran and The Prophet (SAW)'s sayings. This spiritual part of the quest for knowledge is what makes science Islamic. In addition, the moral context of Islam guides the type of research as a distinctive Islamic element in the study of nature and life. Indeed, the search for science in Islam is not an end but a means to finding the truth that draws us closer to the Power and Wisdom of Allah (SWT).

In fact, just as Muslim scientists read the Holy Quran as the "revealed book" of signs (Ayat) from Allah (SWT), they are also supposed to consider the universe as a "divine open book" containing His signs (Ayat). Therefore, scientific discoveries in nature complement Quranic teachings and enhance faith. Consequently, the scientific observer of nature is a kind of wise seeker of truth in the act of worship, as Allah (SWT) says

"Those who remember Allah while standing, sitting, or (reclining) on their backs, and reflect in the creation of the heavens and the Earth, (saying) 'Our Lord! You have not created this in vain. Glory to You! Save us, then, from the chastisement of the Fire"

(Quran 3:191).

Muslim scholars of the Golden Age of the Islamic civilization were keenly aware of these signs (Ayat) and the description of the universe given by Allah (SWT) in this Quranic verse and were deeply fascinated by them. Consequently, Muslim scientists of the Muslim civilization greatly influenced modern science.

Ibn Al-Haytham

Among the towering figures of Islam's Golden Age, Ibn Al-Haytham (965-1040 CE) revolutionized mathematics, astronomy, and physics through rigorous methodology. As a dedicated truth-seeker, he established principles of scientific inquiry that remain relevant today: *"The duty of the man who investigates the writings of scientists, if learning the truth is his goal, is to make himself an enemy of all that he reads and attack it from every side. He should also suspect himself as he performs his critical examination of it, so that he may avoid falling into either prejudice or leniency."* This approach demonstrated how Islamic values of truth-seeking transformed scientific methodology. Recognized as the father of modern optics, Ibn Al-Haytham fundamentally transformed understanding of vision and light. His masterwork, the *"Kitab al-Manazir"* (Book of Optics), written between 1011-1021, influenced European science for centuries through its Latin translation. During the Scientific Revolution, giants like Newton, Kepler, Huygens, and Galileo regularly cited his work, demonstrating how Islamic scholarship laid foundations for later European scientific development. Ibn Al-Haytham was also the first to explain the theory of vision correctly and to argue that vision occurs in the brain, highlighting observations that it is subjective and affected by personal experience. He also demonstrated through experiments that light travels in a straight line, and carried out various experiments with lenses, mirrors, refraction and reflection.

His analyses of reflection and refraction take separate account of the vertical and horizontal components of light rays. He was the first physicist to give a complete statement of the law of reflection. He was also the first to assert that the incident ray, the reflected ray, and the surface normal all lie in the same plane perpendicular to the plane of reflection. Occasional references to theology or religious sentiment can also be found in his technical works, for example, in Doubts Concerning Ptolemy: Truth is sought for its own sake. Truth is hard to find, and the road to it is full of pitfalls. Allah (SWT), however, has not preserved the scientist from error and has not preserved science from defects and faults. Had this been the case, scientists would not have disagreed on any point of science.

Medieval biographers credit Ibn Al-Haytham with over 200 works spanning diverse scientific fields, with 96 documented scientific treatises. While most have been lost to history, more than 50 survive in various forms, revealing the breadth of his genius: nearly half address mathematics, 23 focus on astronomy, 14 on optics, and others cover various scientific disciplines. This prolific output demonstrates the comprehensive scientific culture fostered by Islamic civilization. In 2014, the episode "Hiding in the Light" of Cosmos: A Spacetime Odyssey, presented by Neil deGrasse Tyson, focused on the achievements of Ibn Al-Haytham. UNESCO declared 2015 the International Year of Light, and its Director-General Irina Bokova called Ibn Al-Haytham the "father of optics". The aim was to celebrate Ibn Al-Haytham's achievements in optics, mathematics, and astronomy. An international campaign, created by the 1001 Inventions organization, entitled 1001 Inventions and the World of Ibn Al-Haytham, featured a series of interactive exhibitions, workshops, and live performances about his work, in partnership with science centers, science festivals, museums, and educational institutions, as well as digital and social media platforms. The campaign also produced and broadcast the short educational film 1001 Inventions and the world of Ibn Al-Haytham.

Divine Revelation

"And build the Ark under Our 'watchful' Eyes and directions"

(Quran 11: 37)

Divine revelation served as the primary source of knowledge for Allah's messengers, including technical and scientific instruction. This verse illustrates how Allah commanded Prophet Noah (AS) to construct the Ark for salvation from the great flood. According to authentic hadiths, the Angel Gabriel provided detailed shipbuilding instructions through revelation, demonstrating how divine guidance encompasses both spiritual and practical knowledge. Historical accounts describe the Ark's impressive dimensions: approximately three hundred yards long, fifty yards wide, and thirty yards high - comparable to modern large vessels. The use of specific materials like wood from the Saul tree (Shorea robusta) shows the precision of divine instruction in practical matters.

Mathematics in Islam

"The sun and the moon [move] are calculated"

(Quran 55 :5)

This verse highlights the sun and moon because all universal life depends on their precisely calculated orbital movements. These celestial bodies maintain perfect sequences according to divine mathematical principles, never deviating even by fractions of seconds across billions of years of cosmic history. This astronomical precision inspired Islamic mathematicians during the Golden Age (8th-12th centuries) to develop sophisticated mathematical tools for understanding and predicting celestial phenomena, recognizing mathematics as the language through which Allah's cosmic design becomes comprehensible to human intellect.

"He Who created the seven heavens one above another: No want of proportion wilt thou see in the Creation of (Allah) Most Gracious. So turn thy vision again: seest thou any flaw?

(Quran 67:3)

Since the universe operates through precise divine calculations, the Quran naturally employs mathematical principles in its very structure. Allah's challenge to produce anything resembling the Quran extends beyond literary beauty to include its mathematical architecture. Quranic verses demonstrate intricate numerical relationships and word patterns that create a mathematical matrix underlying the text's spiritual message. This mathematical dimension provides additional evidence of divine authorship, as such complex numerical relationships could not result from human composition. An example of this is the number 19, which appears only once in the entire Quran which is the chapter 74 (Al Mudhateer), while talking about the angels of punishment, and that there are 19 angels in charge of the fire of Hell, the Blessed and Exalted says: *"There are nineteen of them "(Quran 74:30).* Why did Allah (SWT) make their number nineteen, neither more nor less? The verse following this one answers this question and confirms that this number has a great secret behind it. It is a trial for the disbelievers, and at the same time, it is a means to increase the faith of the believers. Therefore, Allah (SWT) says: *"And We did not make their number except as a trial for those who disbelieved" (Quran 74:31).* Then He mentioned to us the other goal, saying: *"And those who believe will increase in faith" (Quran 74: 31).* Then Allah (SWT) confirmed that this number is a means of remembrance and a reminder to humanity that the Quran is the truth. Therefore, He said: *"And it is only a reminder to mankind." (Quran 74: 31).* After that, Allah (SWT) swore that this number represents one of the greatest miracles. Therefore, He said after that: "Indeed, it is one of the greatest"

(Quran 74: 35).

Another miracle is that the number of Surah Al-Muddaththir is 74, and that the miracle of the number 19 was discovered in 1974. It was discovered that the entire structure of the Quran is mathematically composed of the symbol number 19. Some examples of how the Holy Quran is coded with the number 19 are:

1. First, the number of Quranic verses in the Quran is 114 = 19 x 6.

2. The number of verses in the Quran is 6,346 = 19 x 334.

3. The number of times the word Allah is mentioned in the Quran is 2,698 = 19 x 142.

4. If we count all the verses where the word Allah occurs that number is 118,123 = 19 x 6,217.

5. The Basmala (bismi ʾllāhi ʾr-raḥmāni ʾr-raḥīmi), the Quranic opening formula, which, with one exception, is at the beginning of every Surah of the Quran, consists of exactly 19 letters.

6. The first word of the Basmala, Ism (name), without contraction, occurs 19 times in the Quran (19×1). [Also, no plural forms, or those with pronoun endings]

7. The second word of the Basmala, Allah (God), occurs 2698 times (19×142).

8. The third word of the Basmala, Rahman (Gracious), occurs 57 times (19×3).

9. The fourth word of the Basmala, Rahim (Merciful), occurs 114 times (19×6).

10. The multiplication factors of the words of the Basmala (1+142+3+6) give 152 (19×8).

11. The Basmala appears 114 times (despite its absence in chapter 9, it appears twice in chapter 27); 114 is 19×6.

12. From the missing Basmala in chapter 9 to the additional Basmala in chapter 27, there are exactly 19 chapters.

13. The occurrence of the additional Basmala is in Quranic verse 27:30. Adding this chapter number and the verse number gives 57 (19×3).

Here are a few more examples of mathematical balance in the Holy Quran:

1. The word "Salawat" (prayers) is mentioned 5 times in the Quran, and the number of daily prayers mandatory for every Muslim is Al- Subh, Al-Duhr, Al-Asr, Al-Maghrib, Al-Isha.

2. The Word "Shahr" (month) is mentioned 12 times in the Quran, just as the number of months there are in a year.

3. The word "Yawm" (day), in the singular, is mentioned 365 times in the Quran, just as the number of days there are in a year.

4. The word "Ayyam" (days), in the plural, is mentioned 30 times in the Quran, just as the number of days there are in a month.

"And of everything We have created pairs, that you may remember"

(Quran 51:49)

Based on this Quranic verse, some pairs are also mentioned equally in the Holy Quran:

1. "Al Hayat" (life) and "Al Mawt" (death) are both mentioned 145 times.

2. "Al-Dunya" (mundane life) and "al Akhira" (the afterlife): both 115 times.

3. "Malaika" (angels) and "Shayatin" (demons): both mentioned 88 times.

4. "Ar Rajul (man) and "Al Mar'a (woman): are both mentioned 24 times.

5. "Ar Raghba (wish) and "al Khauf (fear): are both mentioned 8 times.

6. As Salihat (good deeds) and "As Sayyi'at" (wrongdoings), both mentioned 167 times.

7. "An Nafaa" (benefit) and "Al Fasad (corruption): both are mentioned 50 times.

Now, when the Prophet (SAW) was asked by the people of Quraish about Allah (SWT), the answer came directly from Him in the form of Chapter 112 of the Noble Quran, which is considered the essence of the unity or the motto of Allah (SWT) 's Oneness (Al Tawheed). "Say (O Muhammad) He is God the One God, the Everlasting Refuge, who has not begotten, nor has been begotten, and equal to Him is not anyone."

(Quran; 112).

This is one of the shortest Chapter of the Holy Quran. Its number of verses is only 4. Let's check the mathematical balance in this Chapter:

1. It has 15 Arabic words. 7 words at the beginning, 7 words at the end, a word in the middle– balance!

2. The number of letters in the first 7 words is 22. The number of letters in the last 7 words is 22! –Balance again!

3. The middle word has three letters. The middle letter is 'lam', which is the 23rd letter of the Arabic alphabet. And there are exactly 23 letters before and after the letter 'lam'! That is, balance!

4. There is another balance! At the end of the first verse, there is the word 'Ahad', and at the end of the last verse, there is also the word 'Ahad'. The word 'Ahad' means the oneness of God.

5. In the middle of the surah, there are words about giving birth. Giving birth is a human characteristic. That means the two sides of the surah are the attributes of Allah (SWT), and the middle is the attributes of humans.

6. As we saw, the middle letter of the Surah is 'Lam' which is the 23rd letter of the Arabic alphabet, and there are exactly 23 letters before and after the 'Lam'. So, the question is, why are there 23 in the middle? The importance of the number 23 is that the number of human chromosomes is 23 pairs, and the middle of the surah deals with the human characteristics of giving birth.

Muslim Mathematicians

"It is Him who has made the sun radiant and the moon luminous and has appointed for the moon certain phases so that you may compute the number of years and other reckonings. God has

created them for a genuine purpose. He explains the evidence (of His existence) to the people of knowledge"

(Quran 10:5)

This verse calls Muslim scientists to study celestial bodies for calculating time periods essential to Islamic practice. Mathematics became crucial for determining prayer times, identifying Ramadan's beginning, and coordinating pilgrimage schedules. During Islam's Golden Age, mathematical sciences flourished as scholars recognized their instrumental role in fulfilling religious obligations while advancing human knowledge. Islamic mathematicians viewed their work as both a practical necessity and a spiritual service. Muslim mathematicians were able to draw on and fuse together the mathematical developments of both Greece and India. Indeed, just after the founding of the House of Wisdom in Baghdad around 810, work started on translating the major Greek and Indian mathematical and astronomy works into Arabic language. Moreover, in the field of geometry, one consequence of the Islamic prohibition on depicting the human form was the extensive use of complex geometric patterns to decorate their buildings, raising mathematics to the form of an art. Over time, Muslim Mathematicians discovered all the different forms of symmetry that can be depicted on a 2-dimensional surface.

From the large number of Muslim Mathematicians of the Golden Age, Muhammad ibn Musa al-Khwarizmi (c. 780-850 CE) earned recognition as the 'Father of Algebra' through groundbreaking mathematical innovations. As director of Baghdad's House of Wisdom, he revolutionized mathematics by:

Advocating the Hindu-Arabic numeral system (0-9): He recognized these numerals' computational power and efficiency, leading to their adoption throughout the Islamic world and later Europe.

Developing algebra: His work, 'Hisab al-Jabr wa'l-Muqabalah', introduced systematic methods for solving polynomial equations, giving algebra its name from 'al-jabr' (restoration/completion).

Discovering zero's significance: Al-Khwarizmi elevated zero from a mere placeholder to a full numeral, enabling negative numbers and advanced calculations impossible under previous systems.

His mathematical innovations transformed computation from cumbersome procedures into elegant, systematic methods that remain foundational to modern mathematics.

Another Muslim mathematician, Omar Khayyam (1048-1131 AD), excelled in mathematics, and among his most prominent achievements in it are the following: (1) He found a method for extracting roots of the third degree. (2) He solved cubic equations by calculating conic sections. (3) He studied Euclid's parallel postulates. (4) He developed Euclid's theory regarding rational numbers by solving the problem of irrational numbers, as he imagined that the number system is broader. Many of those that were used in the past, and he succeeded in attributing them to real numbers. In the 10th Century, another Muslim mathematician, called Muhammad Al-Karaji, worked to extend algebra still further, freeing it from its geometrical heritage, and introduced the theory of algebraic calculus. Among other things, Al-Karaji used mathematical induction to prove the binomial theorem. A binomial is a simple type of algebraic expression that has just two terms, which are operated on only by addition, subtraction, multiplication, and positive whole-number exponents, such as $(x + y)^2$. The coefficients needed when a binomial is expanded form a symmetrical triangle, usually referred to as Pascal's Triangle after the 17th-century French mathematician Blaise Pascal, although many other mathematicians had studied it centuries before him in India, Persia, China, and Italy, including Al-Karaji.

Moreover, the 13th-century Muslim astronomer, scientist, and mathematician Nasir Al-Din Al-Tusi was perhaps the first to treat trigonometry as a separate mathematical discipline, distinct from astronomy. Building on earlier work by Greek mathematicians such as Menelaus of Alexandria and Indian work on the sine function, he gave the first extensive exposition of spherical trigonometry, including listing the six distinct cases of a right triangle in spherical trigonometry. One of his major mathematical contributions was the formulation of the famous law of sines for plane triangles.

Furthermore, one of the most remarkable Muslim mathematicians was Ghiyath Al-Din Al-Kashani, who thrived in the late 14th Century. His focus was on the theory of numbers and the techniques of computations. In 1424, he astounded the mathematical world by calculating a value of 2π to an unprecedented sixteen decimal digits of accuracy, a feat that still stands as a testament to his mathematical precision. He achieved this by using an approximation of the circle with 805306368-sided polygons. His magnum opus, "Miftah-Ul-Hissab" or "The Calculator's Key", introduced an algorithm for finding the fifth root of any number. This groundbreaking book was a staple in Persian schools until the 17th Century. Kashani's contributions also extended to trigonometry, where he devised a method to approximate the function "sin" by solving a cubic equation with remarkable precision.

Natural Sciences in Islam

"It is He to whom belongs the dominion over the heavens and the Earth, and who has not taken a son and has no associate in His dominion, for He has created all things according to precise measures"

(Quran 25:2)

After introducing Islam's contribution to the universal scientific language of mathematics, the focus now shifts to natural sciences, which is a branch of science that seeks to understand the divine laws governing the natural world using experimental and scientific methods. It is a branch of science that is concerned with describing, understanding, and predicting natural phenomena, based on empirical evidence derived from observation and experimentation. As shown in the figure, the natural sciences can be divided into three main branches.

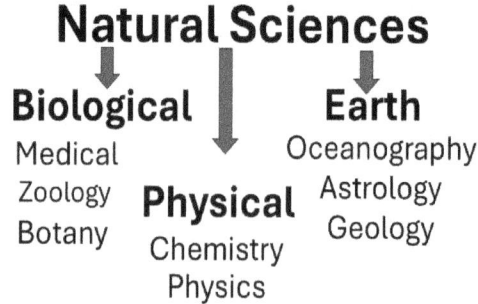

We will discuss some aspects of the physical, biological, and earth sciences presented in the Holy Quran and the hadiths of the Prophet (SAW), in addition to the corresponding contributions of Muslim scholars during the golden age of Islamic civilization.

Natural Sciences

Physics and chemistry, although somewhat similar, are completely different. The main difference here is that physics is concerned with the study of the universe, while chemistry is the study of chemicals, chemical reactions, and individual molecules.

For physical sciences consult the following verse.

"He has created everything, and has measured it exactly according to its due to precise measurements (Faqaddarah Taqdeera)"

(Quran 25:2)

According to this Quranic verse, "Faqaddarah Taqdeera" means precise measurements and calculations. It is worth noting that the name of Allah (SWT), "The Dominant (Al-Muqtadir)", means that He exercises His authority over everything in the universe. This means that the quantity, time, and place of anything are determined by precise calculations based on certain divine laws and divine forces.

Physics in the Quran

Building upon earlier discussions of birds in flight, fish swimming, and celestial movements, we now explore additional physical phenomena described in the Quran. These verses demonstrate how Allah embedded scientific insights within spiritual guidance, inviting believers to contemplate the physical laws governing creation while strengthening their faith through observation and reflection.

107

"Whoever does work of an atom's weight of good will see it. And whoever does work of an atom's weight of evil will see it"

(Quran 99:7-8)

The Quranic reference to 'work' carries both spiritual and physical significance. While the verse primarily addresses moral accountability, it also reflects physical reality: in physics, work represents force applied through distance. When the Quran links work to 'weight,' it resonates with gravitational physics. An object with mass (m) falling under Earth's gravity (g) performs work (W) equal to gravitational force (mg) multiplied by distance (Δh): $W = mg \times \Delta h$. This mathematical relationship underlies countless natural processes, from rainfall to planetary motion.

$$W = F_g \Delta h = mg\Delta h \qquad (14)$$

"Do you bring it down (in rain) from the cloud, or do We?"

(Quran 56:69)

On the same subject of work and weight, this Quranic verse relates to the divine law of charity of the previous chapter, as the water falling in the water cycle is described:

$$\text{Precipitation } (WF) \propto \frac{(PE_{High} - PE_{low})}{R_{air}} \left(\frac{Driving\ force}{Resistance} \right) \qquad (13)$$

Based on the law of divine creation in pairs, the presence of air resistance (R_{air}) in the denominator of the equation indicates that it creates a force opposite to the weight of the falling drop, and by the

108

mercy of Allah (SWT), this causes friction that slows down the speed of the raindrops. Thus, the kinetic energy of the falling raindrops decreases; otherwise, they will destroy and kill everything on Earth.

> *"Allah is the Light of the heavens and the earth. His light is like a niche in which there is a lamp, the lamp is in a crystal, the crystal is like a shining star"*
>
> (Quran 24:35)

This Quranic verse is a divine sign that objects can be seen because they are hit by light, then the light is reflected, so that we can see objects around us. Physically, Allah (SWT) illuminates the earth and the sky with the sun. The sun has an average distance of 149.6 million kilometers from the Earth. Moreover, the Quranic verse also indicates that since, electromagnetic waves do not require a medium for their propagation and since light is an electromagnetic wave, light can travel in a vacuum and reach the earth's surface at the speed of light of 3×10^8 m/s.

> *"And whomsoever He wills to send astray, He makes his breast closed and constricted, as if he is climbing up to the sky"*
>
> (Quran 6:125)

This is one of the examples of the scientific miracles in the Noble Quran, because no one flew in the sky during the time of the Prophet (SAW). This can be explained scientifically by the fact that when we ascend to the sky, we face greater difficulties in breathing. This is scientifically explained by the effect of Earth's gravity on the density of the air. Indeed, the density of the air (and therefore the amount of oxygen) is less when we ascend into the sky, and we breathe with greater difficulty.

> "He arranges [each] matter from the heaven to the earth; then it will ascend to Him in a Day, the extent of which is a thousand years of those which you count."

(Quran 32:5)

1400 years ago, no one knew the speed of light, but there is a scientific sign in this Quranic verse. Since Allah (SWT) created the angels from light, they have a very low density. They move at any speed, from zero to the speed of light, and the angels are the ones who carry out Allah (SWT)'s commands. In this Quranic verse, Allah (SWT) specifies 1,000 years of what they counted (not what they traveled). As Muslims are accustomed to following the lunar calendar, each year consists of 12 lunar months, and therefore the angels travel in one day a distance of 1000 years of what they counted (the moon). Since this Quranic verse refers to distance, Allah (SWT) says that the angels travel in one day the same distance that the moon travels in 12,000 lunar cycles. It turns out that in an inertial geocentric framework, 12,000 lunar orbits/Earth's day is equal to the speed of light.

> "And even if We opened to them a gate from the sky and they were to continue ascending thereto, they would only say: "Our

eyes have been intoxicated: Nay, we have been bewitched by sorcery."

(Quran 15:14-15)

Finally, to explain this Quranic verse, they reach the dark space, and they cannot see because there is very little matter that reflects or reflects the sunlight. However, on Earth, when sunlight passes through our atmosphere, many molecules and particles scatter the sunlight and make the sky blue during the day.

Muslim Physicists

"It is He, Who has created for you (the sense of) hearing (ears), sight (eyes), and hearts (understanding). "Yet, only few of you are grateful"

(Quran 23 :78)

This verse reveals Allah's gift of sight as a tool for both physical observation and spiritual reflection. The Quran contains 34 verses addressing visual function, demonstrating the text's attention to this crucial sense. References to 'eye/eyes' (15 times), 'light' (8 times), 'see' (3 times), 'sight' (7 times), and 'vision' (1 time) underscore vision's importance in Islamic epistemology. This Quranic emphasis on sight naturally led Muslim scholars to pioneer the science of optics during Islam's Golden Age. In this topic, the science of optics studies the nature of vision and investigates the principles of the propagation, reflection, and refraction of light.

Optics became a central discipline during the Islamic civilization's Golden Age. While earlier Greek and ancient civilizations studied vision, they held contradictory theories: the 'intromission' theory proposed that visual forms enter the eye from objects, while the 'emission' theory suggested that eyes emit rays to perceive objects. These competing explanations created confusion that persisted until Islamic scholars applied rigorous experimental methods to resolve the debate definitively. Research continued in the field of Optics around the same theories and without any advances until the Islamic civilization. The Muslims' contributions had a different, advanced, and unique approach. The reason was that Muslims were proficient in several fields of science related to Optics like Astronomy, Geometry, Mechanics and others. For example, while Ibn Al-Haytham gained fame throughout the Islamic world as a mathematician and astronomer, his revolutionary 'Kitab al-Manazir' (Book of Optics) became his most influential work in Europe. This masterpiece earned him George Sarton's acclaim as 'the greatest Muslim physicist and one of the greatest students of optics of all time.' His experimental approach to vision fundamentally transformed European understanding of light and sight, influencing giants like Newton, Kepler, and Galileo.

Ibn Al-Haytham showed here that if the moon behaved like a mirror, the light it receives from the sun would be reflected at a given point on the Earth from a smaller part of its surface than is observed. He accordingly argued that the moon sends out its borrowed light in the same manner as a self-luminous source, that is, from every point on its surface in all directions. This was confirmed using an astronomical diopter having a slit of variable length through which various parts of the moon could be viewed from an opposite hole in a screen parallel to the slit.

Ibn Al-Haytham and his student Kamal al-Din pioneered the camera obscura, making groundbreaking observations of this optical phenomenon. The camera obscura ('dark chamber') consists of a darkened room or box with a small hole allowing light to project inverted images of external scenes onto the opposite wall. This device revealed fundamental principles of light behavior and image formation, laying the conceptual foundation for modern photography and cinematography. In the 11th Century, Al-Haytham determined virtually everything Newton advanced regarding optics centuries prior and is regarded by numerous authorities as the "founder of optics." Al-Haytham was the most quoted physicist of the Middle Ages. His works were 7806 and quoted by many European scholars during the 16th and 17th Centuries than those of Newton and Galileo combined.

> *"And it is He who placed for you the stars that you may be guided by them through the darknesses of the land and sea. We have detailed the signs for a people who know"*
>
> (Quran 6:97)

The Islamic understanding of the astronomical model was based on the Greek Ptolemaic system. However, many early astronomers began to question the system, as it was not always accurate in its predictions and was very complex because astronomers were trying to mathematically describe the motion of celestial bodies. Ibn al-Haytham published "Doubt on Ptolemy," which summarized his numerous criticisms of the Ptolemaic model. This book encouraged other astronomers to develop new models to explain celestial motion better than Ptolemy. In Ibn al-Haytham's Book of Optics, he argues that the celestial spheres were not made of solid matter and that air in the sky is less dense than this atmospheric air. Al-Haytham ultimately concluded that celestial bodies follow the same laws of physics as terrestrial bodies.

> *"And of His signs are the ships in the sea, like mountains. If He willed, He could still the wind, and they would remain motionless on its surface. Indeed, there are signs for every patient and grateful"*
>
> (Quran 42: 32-33)

In the field of mechanics, John the Grammarian rejected the Aristotelian view of motion and argued that a thing acquires a tendency to move when it has a motive force acting on it. In the eleventh century, Ibn Sina roughly adopted this idea, believing the moving object has a force that is dissipated by external factors such as air resistance. Ibn Sina distinguished between "force" and "inclination," and claimed that a thing may acquire it when the object is in opposition to its natural movement. Therefore, he concluded that the continuation of the movement is due to the inclination that is transmitted to the being, and that this being will be in a state of movement until the inclinations are spent. He also claimed that the projectile in a vacuum will not stop unless acted upon. This concept of motion is consistent with the more recent Newton's first law of motion (inertia), which states that a moving body will remain in motion unless acted upon by an external force.

Finally, Abu Al Aziz ibn Ismail Al-Jazari, who was born in northern Syria in 1136 AD, is one of the Muslim scholars who is considered one of the greatest engineers in the history of humanity. His inventions contributed to the emergence of many intelligent machines, and he was the first to create robots in the world. Al-Jazari presented me with his immortal book "The Combining Knowledge and Useful Action in the Art of Tricks." He spent 25 years writing this book, which provides a detailed, diagrammatic explanation of how each machine works. This book has been translated into English and several other languages, and from it, the West has learned everything it knows today about engineering and artificial intelligence. One of Al-Jazari's most important inventions was the ablution robot, which he presented to King Amir, the Emir of Diyar Bakr, who asked Al-Jazari to make him a machine that would spare him the need for servants whenever he wanted to perform ablution for prayers.

Chemistry in the Quran

"We sent down iron - in which there is strong power and benefit for the people"

(Quran 57:25)

Metals comprise approximately three-quarters of known chemical elements, with aluminum, iron, calcium, sodium, potassium, and magnesium dominating Earth's crust. While most metals exist within mineral ores due to their reactive nature, noble metals like gold, silver, platinum, and copper often occur naturally in pure form. This Quranic verse reveals iron's extraterrestrial origin: *'We sent down iron'* aligns remarkably with modern astrophysics, showing that iron forms within massive stars and reaches Earth through supernova explosions and cosmic processes. All iron throughout our solar system originated from stellar sources, as our Sun lacks the necessary conditions for iron synthesis. While the Sun's surface reaches 6,000° C and its core approximately 20 million °C, iron formation requires temperatures exceeding 100 million °C, found only in massive stars. When these stellar giants exhaust their nuclear fuel, they explode as supernovae, dispersing iron-enriched material throughout space, eventually forming new planetary systems like ours. When the amount of iron exceeds a certain level in a star, the star can no longer accommodate it, and it eventually explodes in what is called a "nova" or a "supernova." These explosions make it possible for iron to be given off into space.

"Bring me sheets of iron" – until, when he had leveled [them] between the two mountain walls, he said, "Blow [with bellows]," until when he had made it [like] fire, he said, "Bring me, that I may pour over it molten copper."

(Quran 18:96)

116

In this Quranic verse, Allah (SWT) describes how iron can be used and even mentions the formation of iron and copper alloys. This verse is consistent with modern methods of processing iron, although they are more modern and advanced today. The principle behind the process of melting, burning, and pouring iron is similar to that described in this Quranic verse.

"There will be sent upon you a flame of fire and smoke, and you will not defend yourselves"

(Quran 55:35)

According to this Quranic verse, when the core of the Red Super giant eventually changed into iron, the nuclear fusion will cease to function since the nuclear structure of iron does not allow its fusion to heavier elements, as this fusion requires the input of excessive quantities of energy. Consequently, the Red Supergiant explodes in the form of a Supernova, the iron core is shattered to pieces that fly out into space, where the nuclei of isotopes with masses heavier than iron are created by the neutron bombardment. As the atomic number of copper is (29) and its atomic weight is (63.546) compared to (26) and (55.58) for iron, respectively, copper is created in outer space by the bombardment of iron nuclei with neutrons.

Spaceships are constantly bombarded by these copper nuclei on their way to outer space and on their return to Earth. The attached copper nuclei react with both humidity and carbon dioxide in the lower atmosphere to change into copper carbonate. This fact was only discovered with space travel in the middle of the 20ᵗʰ century. The Quranic verses related to iron and cupper are therefore a living testimony for both the holy Quran and the Prophethood of the Noble Messenger who received it.

Muslim Chemists

Muslim scientists revolutionized chemistry by separating empirical investigation from mystical practices. While ancient alchemy relied on Aristotelian four-element theory (earth, air, fire, water) mixed with occult beliefs, Islamic scholars established chemistry as a rigorous experimental science. They distinguished between legitimate chemical processes and fraudulent alchemical claims, laying foundations for modern scientific methodology. For example, in a famous chapter of his Muqaddima (Prolegomena), Ibn Khaldun thus denounced as fraudulent the practice of applying a thin layer of gold on top of silver jewelry, as one of many perversions in the use of metals. For him, the Divine Wisdom wanted gold and silver to be rare metals to guarantee profit and wealth. Their disproportionate growth would make transactions useless and would "run contrary to such wisdom".

Centuries before Ibn Khaldun, Al-Kindi also wrote specifically against such transmutations, warning against alchemists transforming ordinary stones into precious stones. Al-Kindi's work is in fact adequately titled Kitab At-Tanbih 'al Khata' Al-Kimiyyawiyyin (the book for warning against the Alchemists). It was Al-Kindi who distinguished alchemy (as the exclusive pursuit of transmutation of the baser metals) from its more respectable sister, chemistry. Considering the time of Al-Kindi, this distinction must be regarded as quite a remarkable achievement.

Jabir ibn Hayyan (8th century) pioneered experimental methodology centuries before its adoption in Europe. His systematic approach included classifying matter into animal, vegetable, and mineral categories, identifying intrinsic properties like temperature and moisture content, and successfully reproducing natural phenomena through controlled laboratory processes. This empirical foundation transformed chemistry from speculative philosophy into experimental science, establishing protocols still fundamental to chemical research today. Even more significant is the knowledge contained in the Latin version of Jabir Ibn Hayyan texts (also known as the Pseudo-Gerber Corpus), which includes the systematic description of numerous chemical processes and reactions, from the synthesis of acids such as nitric and sulphuric to aqua regia, oxides and salts.

In addition, the book details many techniques of chemistry such as precipitation, crystallization, and distillation, and provides instructions for making the apparatus and equipment necessary to carry them out. It also introduces methods for improving the quality of a multitude of manufactured products, such as the production of steel and other metals (and the passivation of their oxidation); the dyeing and waterproofing of cotton and leather; the chemical analysis of pigments and other natural substances; the purification of gold; and the production of pure mercury from cinnabar. His enormous influence that both the original and the Latinized version of his work had on the development of alchemy and its final transmutation into a modern science: chemistry, first in the Islamic world and then, centuries later, in Europe.

Biological and Medical Sciences in Quran

Biological sciences encompass the study of life in all its forms: cellular biology, genetics, reproduction, biodiversity, anatomy, physiology, and ecology. From an Islamic perspective, these sciences reveal Allah's intricate design in living systems, from molecular processes to ecosystem interactions. This section explores medical sciences, zoology, and botany as presented in the Quran and Prophetic traditions, alongside the groundbreaking contributions of Muslim scientists during Islam's Golden Age.

> *"There comes forth from their bellies (of bees) a drink of varying hues. Therein is cure for men. Surely, in that is a Sign for a people who reflect."*

> (Quran 16: 69)

Islam encourages medical research and treatment, viewing healing as both divine mercy and human responsibility. The Prophet (SAW) declared: *'There is no disease that Allah has created, except that He also has created its treatment'* [Sahih al-Bukhari 5678]. This verse specifically mentions honey's curative properties. Modern analysis reveals honey's complex composition: 80-85% carbohydrates, 15-17% water, 0.3% proteins, plus beneficial amino acids, antioxidants, and vitamins that contribute to its antimicrobial and healing properties. In modern times, it has been discovered that honey has antibacterial properties as well as other health benefits. This cure by honey is mentioned by the following Prophet's saying

"A man came to the Prophet (SAW) and said, "My brother has some Abdominal trouble." The Prophet (SAW) said to him "Let him drink honey." The man came for the second time and the Prophet (SAW) said to him, 'Let him drink honey." He came for the third time and the Prophet (SAW) said, "Let him drink honey." He returned again and said, "I have done that ' The Prophet (SAW) then said, "Allah has said the truth, but your brother's brother's brother's abdomen has told a lie. Let him drink honey." So he made him drink honey, and he was cured

[Sahih Al-Bukhari 5684].

"And verily in cattle (too) will you find an instructive Sign. From what is within their bodies, between excretions and blood, We produce, for your drink, milk, pure and agreeable to those who drink it"

(Quran 16:66).

Based on this Quranic verse, the milk production in the female body is one of the most complex creations to understand. In this topic, the Muslim scientist Ibn Nafees described the production of milk around 800 years ago. However, William Harvey introduced this knowledge to

121

the Western world only around 400 years ago. Besides being pure and agreeable, the Prophet (SAW) said

"The milk of the bovine (cow) contains healing, its fat is a medicine, and its meat a cause for sickness."

[authentic hadith: Tabarani].

"And it is He who sends down rain from the sky, and We produce thereby the growth of all things. We produce from it greenery from which We produce grains arranged in layers. And from the palm trees – of its emerging fruit are clusters hanging low. And [We produce] gardens of grapevines and olives and pomegranates, similar yet varied. Look at [each of] its fruit when it yields and [at] its ripening. Indeed, in there are signs for a people who believe"

(Quran 6:99)

Regarding cure based on herbs, there are at least nineteen plants with medicinal applications that have been mentioned in the Holy Quran, such as Camphor, Date palm, Fig, Ginger, Grape, Garlic, Lentil, Olive, Onion, Pomegranate, Summer squash, sweet basil, Athel tamarisk, Toothbrush tree, Arak, Mustard, Acacia, Cucumber, leek, and Cedrus. The phototherapeutic benefits of some of these nineteen medicinal plants were supported by numerous scientific publications. "The Earth has been made for me a Masjid (place for praying) and a thing to purify." [Sahih al-Bukhari 438].

Based on this hadith, the production of antibiotics from soil could save life of millions of people: Indeed, global deaths from antibiotic-resistant infections are predicted to hit 10 million a year by 2050. It is well known today that antibiotics are substances that can stop or slow the growth of certain living (biotic) microbes, such as bacteria. Penicillin is probably the most famous strain of antibiotic. In this topic, when the British scientist Alexander Fleming returned from vacation to find that one of the petri dishes was covered in a bacteria-killing mold. He had discovered penicillin, the world's first antibiotic. However, today humanity is facing an antibiotic crisis. Superbugs have evolved resistance to dozens of drugs in doctors' arsenals, leading to infections that are increasingly difficult to treat.

In concordance with this Prophet (SAW)'s saying, scientists discovered that there are some kinds of soil that can remove the most obstinate types of bacteria. Today, scientists are looking to manufacture a killer for the most obstinate kind of bacteria extracted from soil. Researchers think the new microbes used as antibiotics are part of soil's microbiome. Billions of identified and unidentified bacteria, fungi, and even microscopic animals make up the living (or once-living) parts of a thriving ecosystem of dirt.

For example, microbiologist Sean Brady reported in 2018 the discovery of a new class of antibiotics extracted from unknown microorganisms living in the soil. This class, which they call "Malacidins", kills several superbugs, including the dreaded methicillin-resistant Staphylococcus aureus (MRSA) without engendering resistance.

Man We did create from a quintessence (of clay); then We placed him as (a drop of) sperm in a place of rest firmly fixed; then We made the sperm into a clot of congealed blood; then of that clot We made a (foetus) lump; then We made out of that lump bones and clothed the bones with flesh; then We developed out of it another creature: so blessed be Allah the Best to create

(Quran 23:12-14)

Modern embryological research has drawn attention to Quranic descriptions of human development. This verse provides a systematic account of embryonic stages that corresponds remarkably with contemporary understanding of fetal development. The Prophet (SAW) elaborated on these stages: *'Each one of you is constituted in the womb of the mother for forty days, and then he becomes a clot of thick blood for a similar period, and then a piece of flesh for a similar period. Then Allah sends an angel who is ordered to write four things: his deeds, his livelihood, his death, and whether he will be blessed or wretched. Then the soul is breathed into him'* [Sahih al-Bukhari 3036]. This hadith describes developmental phases that align with modern embryological timelines.

Based on this hadith, the soul enters the foetus at around 120 days, after conception, the foetus is no longer a mere living organism but a human being. The concept of human development in stages was not widely recognized until later. The description of these stages described in this Quranic verse are:

1. Creation from Clay: Allah (SWT) created human beings from an "extract of clay". This indicates that human beings are formed from the elements of the Earth. This linkage signifies that human body is part of nature.

2. Stages of Development: The Quranic verses describe the various stages of human development. The use of terms such as 'alaqah (a clinging substance) and Muḍġaï (chewed-like lump) reflects the gradual transformation of the embryo during its early stages.

3. Formation of Bones and Flesh: The Quranic indication that bones are formed before being clothed with flesh is in concordance with modern embryological knowledge. Embryos initially develop a skeletal structure before muscle and tissue formation.

4. Growth and Creation: The Quranic notion of growth and creation in successive stages aligns with the biological processes that occur during embryonic development.

Modern embryology began only with the invention of the microscope in the 17th Century. However, only in the late 1950s when ultrasound was first utilized for uterine scanning, was the real developmental chronology of human foetus available. Karl Ernst von Baer along with Heinz Christian Pander, also proposed the germ layer theory of development which helped to explain how the embryo developed in progressive steps. In conclusion, advancements in medical science have enabled researchers to study embryonic development in precise details. Techniques such as ultrasound imaging and molecular biology have provided a deep understanding of the stages of embryogenesis. The resemblance between the Quranic description and modern embryological knowledge is frequently mentioned as a proof that the Holy Quran is the Book of Our Creator (SWT).

"Read in the Name of your Lord Who created. created humans from Alaq"

(Quran 32:7-9)

This Quranic verse is the first revealed word of the Quran where Allah (SWT) inform us that we are created from Alaq. But this Arabic word doesn't have a universally accepted meaning. Could "Alaq" be the genetic chromosomes made from DNA? Some fundamental principles of human genetics mentioned in the Quran and Sunnah are compared to the same knowledge in Western science. In this subject, an allele is an alternative version of a gene that produces a distinctive phenotypic effect. Mendel worked on peas and coined the terms "dominant" and "recessive" traits, which are used to describe alleles. In autosomal transmission, both alleles of a gene must be recessive to express the recessive phenotype whereas a single dominant allele is sufficient for the expression of a dominant phenotype. This also means that a recessive allele can be masked by a dominant allele in one generation but reappear in the next generation.

In the following Prophet (SWA)' saying, the Arabic word `irq" seems to approximate this concept. "A desert Arab came to Allah's Messenger (SAW) and said: My wife has given birth to a dark-complexioned child, and I have disowned him. Thereupon Allah's Apostle (SAW) said: Have you any camels? He said: Yes. He said: What is their color? He said? They are red. He said: Is there anyone dusky among them? He said: Yes. Allah's Messenger (SAW) said: How has it come about? He said: Messenger of Allah, it is perhaps due to the strain [Irq] to which it has reverted, whereupon the Prophet (SAW) said: It (the birth) of the black child may be due to the strain [Irq] to which he (the child) might have reverted." [Sahih Muslim Siddiqui AH, translator. Book 9, Number 3574].

Since Islam advocated justice and human rights and it is genetically possible for two lighter-skinned parents to have a dark-skinned child, understanding genetic possibilities could prevent false accusations of paternity and the resulting abuse against innocent people, especially women.

"And He creates pairs, male and female from a drop when it is deposited"

(Quran 53:45-46)

In the topic related to the sex of the baby, Morgan and Bridges, studying in 1919, the Drosophila fly, discovered that the X and Y

127

chromosomes play an important role in sex determination. However, it wasn't until 1959 that sex determination became known in mammals when Jacobs et al. studied humans, and for Welshons and Russell in their study of the mouse the same year, to show that mammals resemble the Melandrium plant in that the Y chromosome is male sex. This paved the way for the idea that spermatozoa determine the baby's eventual sex by containing either the X or the Y chromosome. The above Quranic verse makes it clear that the sex of the offspring is determined shortly after a drop of sperm is deposited. This is confirmed for emphasis in the following Quranic verse *"For˺ indeed, We ˹alone˺ created humans from a drop of mixed fluids, ˹in order˺ to test them, so We made them hear and see" (Quran 76:2).*

Muslim Doctors & Pharmacists

"You are the best community ever raised for humanity; you encourage good, forbid evil, and believe in Allah"

(Quran 3:110)

While Europe experienced intellectual decline during the early medieval period, the Islamic world became the center of medical and scientific advancement from the 8th century onward. The Islamic Caliphate's commitment to knowledge created unprecedented opportunities for scholars. Institutions like Baghdad's House of Wisdom and similar centers in Damascus, Cordoba, and Cairo fostered medical research, translation of ancient texts, and original discoveries that would influence global medicine for centuries. This culture of patro-nage allowed Islamic scholars of the Golden Age to study and learn, and also translate many Greek texts into Arabic, which helped preserve the wisdom of the Greeks and enabled its transmission to Europe during the Renaissance.

The sheer size of the Islamic empire allowed access to wealth and raw materials for industry and agriculture. This gave the Islamic world the capacity to support a structure of learning and scholarship as the foundation of Islamic contributions to the history of biology and science. Based on the above Quranic verse, Islamic influence spread to various regions as Muslim scholars played a central role in translating and preserving ancient scientific texts but also enhancing them with their own discoveries.

"O mankind, there has to come to you instruction from your Lord and healing for what is in the breasts and guidance and mercy for the believers"

(Quarn 10:57)

Muslim physicians revolutionized medical practice through systematic innovation across multiple domains. Islamic hospitals (Bimaristans) pioneered many features of modern healthcare: specialized departments for different conditions, separate wards for contagious diseases, medical education programs, and pharmacy services. These institutions served patients regardless of social status, religion, or ability to pay, establishing principles of universal healthcare that remain relevant today. They prioritized cleanliness, new technologies, medical training, and advanced procedures and aimed to treat people of all ages and socioeconomic backgrounds. Rooms were designated for each type of illness; most importantly, contagious and non-contagious diseases were separated. Emphasis was placed on personal and institutional hygiene, including the use of alcohol as an antiseptic.

A chief physician headed groups of doctors specializing in each disease. Examinations were held for entry into the medical profession, which significantly elevated and regulated the profession. Influential figures such as Abū-Bakr Muhammad Ibn Zakariya Al-Razi developed chemical devices still used today in pharmaceutical laboratories, such as mortars and pestles, flasks, and vials. He also carefully recorded drug preparation processes such as distillation, evaporation and crystallization.

"And when I am ill, it is He who cures me"

(Quran 26:80)

Moreover, Islamic pharmacology emphasized modern organic chemistry practices such as purity and empiricism. Islamic surgeons were known for performing and documenting novel surgical procedures. They also recorded the complex tools they invented and used. Abū Al-Qāsim Khalaf Ibn Al-'Abbās al-Zahrāwī, known as the "father of surgery", wrote the book "Kitab Al-Tasrif", a detailed illustrated guide that taught subsequent generations of surgical students. Translated into Latin, the book became the leading medical text in European universities during the later Middle Ages. He also improved surgical methods, such as removing kidney stones, to reduce decay rates.

The invention of surgical tools such as syringes, forceps, bone saws, and casts is also attributed to Al-Zahrāwī. He was also the first known doctor to make incisions on his patients' skin, which is still a standard procedure today. Finally, he also pioneered methods of cauterization and suturing.

Additionally, Ibn Al-Nafis, a 13th-century Muslim physician, described the pulmonary circulation more than 300 years before William Harvey. Furthermore, Al-Razi (Rhazes), born in 865, was the most outstanding physician of the Islamic world. He wrote Kitab Al-Mansuri (Liber Almartsoris in Latin), a 10-volume treatise on Greek medicine, and published on smallpox and measles. His texts continued to be reprinted well into the 19th Century. The medical texts of Ibn Rushd (Averroes) were also widely used in European universities.

Finally, Ibn-Sina is one of the most famous and influential scientists in the history of medicine. The Canon of Medicine, which is his most celebrated book in medicine, presents a summary of all the medical knowledge of his time. Ibn-Sina wrote a complete section about kidney calculi in his book. Totally, 65 herbal, eight animal, and four mineral medicines are mentioned in his book as beneficial drugs for dissolving, expelling, and preventing kidney calculi. Ibn-Sina also introduced a very advanced drug designing based on drug delivery, targeting the organ, deposition in the site of action, pain control, wound healing, clearance after action, and supporting the organ. Using

Ibn-Sina's ideas help scientists to choose better drugs with a historical background to reduce the cost of therapies and research projects.

Zoology in Quran

"Allah has created every [living] creature from water. And of them are those that move on their bellies, and of them are those that walk on two legs, and of them are those that walk on four. Allah creates what He wills. Indeed, Allah is over all things competent"

(Quran 24:45)

The Quran frequently references animal life as sources of spiritual reflection and practical wisdom. Current scientific knowledge identifies approximately 38,000 spider species, with estimates suggesting countless more await discovery. This vast biological diversity demonstrates the limitations of human knowledge compared to Allah's infinite creation. For believers, animal behavior and characteristics serve as divine signs (Ayat) revealing deeper truths about existence, morality, and divine wisdom. Indeed, animals inspire us, help us to reflect, teach and guide us, and ultimately let us know a little bit better about the Absolute Power, Wisdom and Knowledge of Our Creator (SWT).

"And there is no creature on [or within] the Earth or bird that flies with its wings except [that they are] communities like you"

(Quran 6:38).

Regarding the topic of animal kingdom, animals are eukaryotic and multicellular organisms. There are millions of species that have been identified; a few share similar characteristics, while others differ drastically. Regarding the place of animals in the Quran, there are more than 200 verses in the Quran dealing with animals and six chapters of the Quran are named after animals or insects: Surat 2, Al Baqarah (The Cow); Surat 6, Al Anaam (The Cattle), Surat 16, Al Nahl (The Bees); Surat 27, Al Naml (The Ants); Surat 29, Al Ankabut (The Spider); and Surat 105, Al-Fil (The Elephant).

"It is God who provided for you all manner of livestock, that you may ride on some of them and from some you may derive your food. And other uses in them for you to satisfy your heart's desires. It is on them, as on ships, that you make your journeys"

(Quran 40:79-80).

As mentioned in this Quranic verse, Allah (SWT) allows human beings to use animals for their own benefit, such as transportation, food, or any other purpose that meets their needs. However, as mentioned in the Quranic verse (6:38), animals are communities like us in the eyes of Allah (SWT). Therefore, they should be treated with the same respect and kindness as human beings, if not more. The Prophet (SAW) also preached to people to show kindness not only to each other but also to all living beings.

"Fear Allah in your treatment of animals," he warned his followers

[Sunan Abu Dawood]

Treating animals with kindness is an act of charity, as the Prophet (SAW) said: "A man walking on a path was very thirsty. Arriving at a well, he went down, drank and came back up. Then he saw a dog with its tongue hanging out, trying to lick mud to quench its thirst. The man said, "This dog has the same thirst as me. » So he went down into the well, filled his shoe with water and gave the dog a drink. Thus, God forgave his sins. "The Prophet was then asked: "Messenger of God, are we rewarded for our kindness to animals? He said: "There is a reward for kindness to any living creature" [Sahih Al-Bukhari and Sahih Muslim]. Moreover, the humane slaughter of animals is strongly supported in the Islamic tradition as the Prophet Muhammad (SAW) said "Verily Allah has enjoined goodness to everything; so, when you kill, kill in a good way and when you slaughter, slaughter in a good way. So, every one of you should sharpen his knife, and let the slaughtered animal die comfortably" [Sahih Muslim (Book 21, Chapter 11, Number 4810].

Finally, it should be noted that, like human beings, animals also glorify and worship Allah (SWT) in their own way, as many verses of the Holy Quran speak of the glorification of creatures such as

"The seven heavens glorify Him, and the Earth and whoever is in them. There is not a thing but celebrates His praise, but you do not understand their glorification"

(Quran 17:44)

"To Allah prostrates whatever is in the heavens and whatever is on the Earth, including animals and angels, and they are not arrogant" (Quran 16:49); and "Have you not regarded that Allah is glorified by everyone in the heavens and the Earth, and the birds spreading their wings. Each knows his prayer and glorification, and Allah knows best what they do"

(Quran 24:41)

Animal societies differ in their organization. Many animals work in teams to help find food and protect themselves. Some of them have a more sophisticated community life than others. They have a distribution of responsibilities, a distribution of tasks, a mutual satisfaction of needs, like organized ant colonies and bee hives.

This verse from the story of Prophet Solomon (AS) reveals remarkable insights about ant behavior: 'Until, when they came upon the valley of the ants, a female ant said, O ants, enter your dwellings that you are not crushed by Solomon and his soldiers while they perceive not' (Quran 27:18). Modern myrmecology (ant study) confirms these observations: among approximately 20,000 known ant species, colonies demonstrate sophisticated communication systems, social organization, environmental awareness, and even predictive responses to threats. The Quranic description anticipates scientific discoveries about ant intelligence, communication abilities, and complex social structures.

The Quran's reference to female ants preceded scientific confirmation by over a millennium. Pierre André Latreille's 1798 research verified that worker ants are indeed female, possessing modified reproductive organs. Ant societies operate as matriarchies: queens establish colonies and focus solely on reproduction, while their daughters (workers) manage all colony operations including foraging, construction, defense, and brood care. This 'sisterhood' creates super-organisms capable of collective decision-making and complex problem-solving. Their tasks range from caring for the queen and the young, foraging, policing conflicts in the colony, and waste.

> *"And your Lord (Allah) revealed to the bees (females): Build your hives in mountains, trees, and in what they build. Then eat (for females) from every fruit and follow (for females) your Lord's enslaved paths, from its bellies exits drink of different colors, in its healing for man. These are signs for those who contemplate"*

(Quran 16:68)

Over 20,000 bee species provide essential pollination services, enabling plant reproduction and maintaining ecosystem balance. Honeybees transfer pollen between flower parts, facilitating seed and fruit development crucial for agricultural crops and natural plant communities. The Quranic chapter An-Nahl (The Bee) demonstrates remarkable numerical patterns: Chapter 16 contains verses with 16 words using 16 different Arabic letters, corresponding to female bees' 16 chromosome pairs and males' 16 individual chromosomes. These mathematical relationships suggest intentional design reflecting divine knowledge of biological systems unknown to 7th-century Arabia.

For the lesson to learn as sign from Allah (SWT), the bee is guided by Allah (SWT) to build its home in the mountains, in trees, and in structures erected by men. Then Allah (SWT) decrees that the bee will have permission to eat from all fruits and to follow the ways which Allah (SWT) has made easy for it, wherever it wants to go in the vast spaces of the wilderness, valleys, and high mountains. Then each bee comes back to its hive without swerving to the right or left, it comes straight back to its home where its offspring and honey are. It makes wax from its wings, and regurgitates honey from its mouth, and lays eggs from its rear, then the next morning it goes out to the fields again.

Secondly, the important fact about bees is that Allah (SWT) mentions the female bees. So, like the ants, female bees are the workers of their community. In 1637, Richard Remnant drafted a paper for the first time that mentioned honeybees are female. For thousands of years prior to this, it was thought that the honeybees are male.

This verse employs the spider as a powerful metaphor:

'The likeness of those who take allies other than Allah is that of the spider. It builds a house, but the most fragile of houses is the spider's house, if they only knew'

137

(Quran 29:41).

The Quran frequently uses natural metaphors to convey spiritual truths, and this comparison reveals multiple layers of meaning. While spider silk possesses remarkable tensile strength (stronger than steel by weight), the web's overall structure remains vulnerable to environmental forces, just as alliances built without divine foundation appear strong but ultimately prove fragile. The spider house in this Quranic verse could be either the life of the family of the spider or the structure of its web. For the life of the family of the spiders, it is well known that spiders are generally solitary creatures, and there are a few reasons for this behavior. First, many spider species are territorial and may become aggressive towards each other if they come into contact. Additionally, spiders often compete for the same resources, such as food and shelter, making it advantageous for them to live alone. It is also proven that in many spider species, females eat the males after sex. This information shows that spiders have weak relationships as they cannot be allies since they compete to survive. However, what is amazing is that the silk of web of spider's web is five times stronger than a strand of steel that is the same thickness. A web made of strands of spider silk as thick as a pencil could stop a Boeing 747 jumbo jet in flight. Scientists still cannot replicate the strength and elasticity of a spider's silk. Spiders have also inspired scientists to make space robots.

Following the pattern with ants and bees, this verse specifically mentions the female spider as web-builder. Arachnological research confirms that female spiders construct and maintain webs as permanent residences serving multiple functions: hunting grounds, mating sites, and nurseries. Females invest considerable energy in web architecture because these structures determine their survival and reproductive success. While females remain largely sedentary within their territories, males typically lead nomadic lives, seeking mates across various female territories, often at considerable personal risk.

This verse addresses potential skepticism about divine attention to seemingly insignificant creatures:

'Allah does not feel shy at mentioning the example of a mosquito, and what is above it'

(Quran 2:26).

Unlike other animals mentioned in the Quran, mosquitoes receive this unique introduction, suggesting their creation contains profound lessons despite their small size. Over 3,700 mosquito species inhabit diverse global environments. While both sexes typically feed on plant nectar, female mosquitoes of many species possess specialized mouthparts for blood feeding, which provides essential proteins for egg production. Like the previous animals cited, Allah (SWT) also mentions a female mosquito in this Quranic verse. Indeed, the high protein and iron content of blood make it essential for reproduction in most mosquito species.

Female mosquitoes possess remarkable anatomical features enabling efficient blood feeding: compound eyes with numerous individual lenses providing wide-angle vision, specialized mandibles and maxillae functioning as piercing instruments, a sophisticated proboscis containing separate channels for saliva injection and blood extraction, and highly sensitive chemoreceptors detecting carbon dioxide, heat, and chemical signatures from potential hosts. Their saliva contains anticoagulants preventing blood clotting during feeding, and they demonstrate host selectivity based on chemical cues, body temperature, and carbon dioxide levels. These amazing facts about female mosquitoes could be the reason Allah (SWT) is not shy to mention the female mosquito in the Holy Quran.

Moreover, Allah (SWT) also says in the same Quranic verse *"and what is above it (female)" (Quran 2:26)*. This Quranic verse is an indication that female mosquitoes have creatures living on their back. Indeed, the strangest discovery by modern science is that there is another very small, microscopic insect living on top of this female Mosquito! In this subject, F.W. Edwards published in 1922 a paper describing a remarkable thing: a flying, biting midge collected from the Malay Peninsula in southeast Asia that he named Culicoides anopheles. What made the midge was remarkable was the thing it bit: Female mosquitoes! So, Allah (SWT) says that mosquitoes have their own parasites.

Muslim Zoologists

"And O my people, this is the she-camel of -Allah – [she is] to you a sign. So let her feed upon -Allah's Earth and do not touch her with harm, or you will be taken by an impending punishment."

140

(Quran 11:64)

Islamic civilization's Golden Age witnessed remarkable zoological achievements driven by both practical necessity and theological motivation. Since Islamic society depended heavily on animals for transportation, agriculture, and trade, systematic animal study became economically essential. More importantly, Islam's theological framework, which views animals as communities with their own forms of worship, encouraged respectful observation and ethical treatment. This unique perspective produced zoological works that integrated empirical observation with spiritual reflection and moral instruction. AL-Jahiz's 'Kitab al-Hayawan' (Book of Animals) stands as medieval Islam's premier zoological work. Rather than merely compiling existing knowledge from Greek, Persian, and Indian sources, Al-Jahiz critically evaluated and expanded upon earlier works, including Aristotle's natural history. His fundamental critique of Aristotelian zoology centered on its purely materialistic approach, which ignored divine purpose in creation. As a devout Muslim scholar, Al-Jahiz pioneered a theological approach to zoology, viewing animal study as a means of recognizing Allah's existence and understanding divine wisdom embedded in natural design. Indeed, Al-Jahiz wrote that one must respect even the smallest natural phenomenon, because the wonders of creation were as visible there as in the greatest of creations: "I would like you to know that a pebble proves the existence of Allah (SWT) is just as much as a mountain, and the human body is as strong proof as the universe. To this end, the small and the light weigh as much as the great and the vast.

The most important book of Muslim zoology after Al-Jahiz's "Kitab Al-Hayawan" is the "Hayat Al-Hayawan Al-Kubra (Great Book on the Life of Animals)" written during 14th Century by Kamal Al-Din Al-Damiri. This enormous work is a systematic study of animals, including information on their religious status according to the Holy Quran, how they should be treated according to Islamic law, traditions regarding their medical benefits for humans, their occult (or magical) properties, and their importance in the interpretation of dreams. Because this text combined religious and scientific perspectives on the study of animals, it became very popular in the Muslim world, even among children. It eventually became a source of folklore as well as a source of inspiration for artists who painted many of the animals described in the text.

Botany in Quran

This oath by sacred plants and places demonstrates botanical significance in Islamic revelation: 'By the fig and the olive. And Mount Sinai. And this safe land'

(Quran 95:1-3).

While numerous Quranic chapters bear animal names (bees, ants, cattle), only Surah At-Tin (The Fig) specifically honors a plant, suggesting the fig's special significance in Islamic tradition. Modern nutritional science validates this distinction: figs provide exceptional dietary fiber, essential minerals, and antioxidants, while their cultivation requires minimal resources, making them ideal sustainable food sources. Today's nutritionists cite many benefits of eating figs. Indeed: (1) Figs are a great source of dietary fiber, which aids in digestion and promotes bowel regularity. (2) They also contain several essential vitamins and minerals, including vitamin A, vitamin K, potassium, and magnesium. (3) Figs also contain high levels of calcium, which helps relax the blood vessels and reduce arterial pressure. This makes figs a great addition to a heart-healthy diet. (4) Figs are also known to contain antioxidants, such as phenols and flavonoids. These compounds help protect the body against oxidative stress and reduce inflammation, which is beneficial for overall health and disease prevention.

The other fruit cited in this Quranic verse is the olive. Many health benefits of eating olives are also mentioned in the literature: (1) The vitamins and antioxidants found in olives may provide important health benefits. (2) Olives are also rich in vitamin E, which can improve skin health and help your immune system. (3) In addition, olives contain the compound oleocanthal, which researchers have shown can kill cancer cells in petri dish experiments. (4) The oleocanthal in olives and olive oil is also linked to a reduced risk for Alzheimer's disease and other brain-related diseases. (5) Olives are also packed with antioxidants, which have been shown to help with chronic inflammation.

In almost all the Middle East and North Africa, caravans consumed a mixture of figs and extra virgin olive oil. They did it regularly because riding for long hours on a camel under the scorching sun day after day can affect your body's health. Finally, in this Quranic verse, Allah (SWT) mentioned the fig before the olive. Today's scholars agree that the domestication of the fig tree came long before the domestication of other fruit crops like grapes, olives, and dates.

This parable illustrates life's transitory nature through botanical processes:

'It is like water that We send down from the sky; the plants of the Earth absorb it; but then it becomes old plants, scattered by the wind'

(Quran 18:45).

The verse accurately describes photosynthesis: plants absorb water, convert it with carbon dioxide into glucose (stored energy), while most water returns to the atmosphere through transpiration. Eventually, plant material decomposes and disperses, completing the cycle. This biological accuracy in a spiritual metaphor demonstrates the Quran's integration of natural observation with moral instruction.

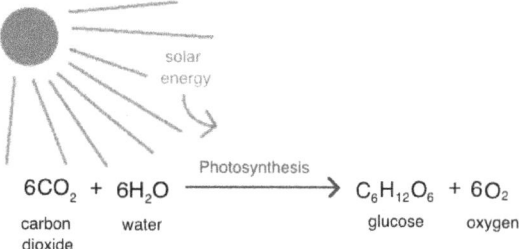

As shown in the Figure, photosynthesis begins when energy from light is absorbed by proteins called reaction centers that contain green chlorophyll (and other colored) pigments/chromophores. Chlorophyll converts carbon dioxide and water into oxygen and sugar. As indicated in this Quranic verse, most of the water evaporates back into the atmosphere while a very small portion remains inside the plant as sugar.

"It is Allah Who splits the grain and the seed. He brings the living from the dead, and He brings the dead from the living. Such is Allah. So how could you deviate?"

(Quran 6:95)

In this Quranic verse, Allah (SWT) says that the seeds are organic matter, and He brings the living from the dead and brings the dead from the living. Today scientists confirm that dead organisms recycle back into living organisms as nutrients recycle back into living organisms. Today we know that it is "the nutrient cycle". The nutrient cycle involves the uptake of nutrients by plants. Then, nutrients are released back into the soil through decomposition. The result is that other plants reabsorb the recycled nutrients (see Figure).

145

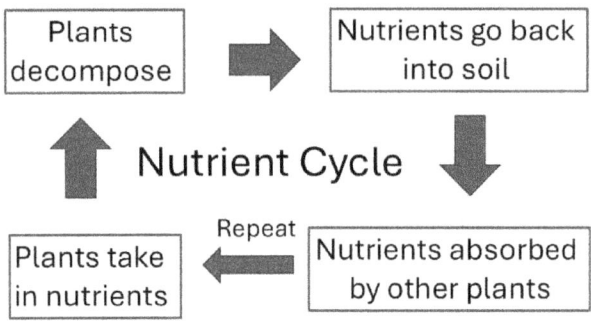

The nutrient cycle is one of the many ways that our planet keeps itself alive. It constantly exchanges inorganic and organic matter back and forth in the environment. Without the nutrient cycle, the remains of dead plants and animals would accumulate on the forest floor and all forest life would collapse because vital compounds would remain tied up in the debris without decomposing.

> *"To Allah, Who created in pairs all things that the Earth produces"*
>
> (Quran 36:36).

In concordance with this Quranic verse, all fruits are based on the existence of male and female organs. Indeed, the botanical science states that every plant has a male and female gender. Even the plants that are unisexual have distinct elements of both male and female. For example, fruits are the end product of the reproduction of the superior plants. The stage preceding fruit is the flower, which has male and female organs (stamens and ovules). Once pollen has been carried to the flower, it bears fruit, which in turn matures and frees its seed.

Muslim Botanists

"And declare (O Muhammad) Quran is guidance and healing for believers"

(Quran 10:57)

Islamic botanical studies emerged from both religious inspiration and practical necessity during the early Golden Age. The compilation of Prophetic Medicine (Al-Tibb al-Nabawi) preserved numerous hadiths describing plant-based remedies for common ailments and dietary guidance. The Quran's frequent botanical references, including descriptions of Paradise's vegetation and plants as signs of divine power, motivated systematic investigation of plant properties. This religious foundation encouraged Muslim scholars to view botanical research as both scientific inquiry and spiritual obligation, leading to comprehensive studies of medicinal and agricultural plants.

Faith-inspired Muslim scholars made groundbreaking contributions to botanical knowledge, developing systematic plant classifications based on propagation methods: cutting propagation, seed germination, and spontaneous generation. Abu Hanifa al-Dinawari (d. 895 CE) deserves recognition as the father of Islamic botany. His masterwork combined Arabic literary tradition with rigorous scientific observation, creating precise botanical terminology so essential that medieval physicians and pharmacists were required to

147

memorize it for professional certification. This integration of artistic expression with scientific accuracy characterized Islamic scholarship's unique approach to natural sciences.

Earlier than Al-Dinawari, were Al-Kindî and Al-Tabari. Al-Tabari's (d. 855) encyclopedic work entitled Firdaws al-Hikma (The Paradise of Wisdom), although including many other sciences such as climatology, astronomy, and philosophy, devotes an important section to botany. Al-Kindî (ca. 800-ca.866) was an innovator in the production of an herbal manual with the main objective of teaching useful botanical pharmacology, as well as toxicology and medicines gained from minerals. His Aqrabadhin (Medical formulary) includes 222 recipes employing at least 319 substances known to Muslim pharmacology in the 9th century.

Moreover, Diyā' Al-Dīn Abū Muhammad 'Abd Allāh Ibn Ahmad Al-Mālaqī, commonly known as Ibn Al-Bayṭār (1197–1248 AD) was a Muslim physician, botanist and pharmacist. His main contribution was to systematically record the additions made by Muslim physicians in the Middle Ages, which added between 300 and 400 types of medicine to the one thousand previously known since antiquity. Ibn Al-Bayṭār learned botany from the Muslim botanist Abū Al-'Abbās Al-Nabātī with whom he started collecting plants in and around Spain. Ibn Al-Bayṭār's largest and most widely read book is his "Compendium on Simple Medicaments and Foods". It is a pharmaceutical encyclopedia listing 1400 plants, foods, and drugs, and their uses. It is organized alphabetically by the name of the useful plant or plant component or other substance, a small minority of the items covered are not botanicals.

Beyond plants used for food and fiber crops, or medicine, gardening was also an important contribution during Muslim rule in the Iberian Peninsula. As in so many other cultural and scientific fields, there was a tendency in the face of huge amounts of evidence to the contrary to ignore or downplay the achievements of Al-Andalus under Muslim rule. This has recently begun to change, and the influence of Islamic gardens and botanists has begun to find recognition. Identification of plants cultivated in Andalusian gardens between the 10th and 15th Centuries can be traced to several main works of botany. One such source is the Cordovan Calendar, an almanac of weather, planting and harvesting times, and Christian holy days. This book dates to the reign of Al-Hakam II, Umayyad ruler of Al-Andalus, between 961 and 976 CE. The Cordovan Calendar lists over one hundred plants.

Earth Sciences in Quran

"Have those who disbelieved not considered that the heavens and the Earth were a joined entity, and We separated them"

(Quran, 21:30)

Earth sciences are the fields of study concerned with the solid Earth, its waters, and the air that envelops it. The fields of study include mainly astronomy, geology, and oceanography. Regarding the creation of the universe, this Quranic verse gives a clear description of its early stages. The skies and the Earth were originally a joined entity. After

149

that, they opened out from this mass to produce the universe in the shape we know today. Contemporary cosmology centers on Big Bang theory, proposing that the universe emerged approximately 13.8 billion years ago from an extremely hot, dense state before expanding and cooling to its current form. Belgian physicist Georges Lemaître first proposed this model in 1927, later supported by Edwin Hubble's observations of galactic recession. The Quranic description of cosmic separation from an initial unified state demonstrates remarkable convergence with this scientific model, suggesting divine revelation anticipated modern cosmological discoveries.

"We built the universe with 'great' might, and We are certainly expanding it "

(Quran 51:47)

This verse finds support in Edwin Hubble's groundbreaking observations that confirmed universal expansion. Hubble's Law ($V = H_0 \times D$) describes how galactic recession velocity increases with distance, where V represents recession velocity, D indicates distance, and H_0 is the Hubble constant. His 1929 observations demonstrated that distant galaxies move away from us at speeds proportional to their distances, providing empirical evidence for cosmic expansion that validates both Big Bang theory and the Quranic description of cosmic separation and expansion. It states that galaxies are moving away from each other at a speed proportional to their distances.

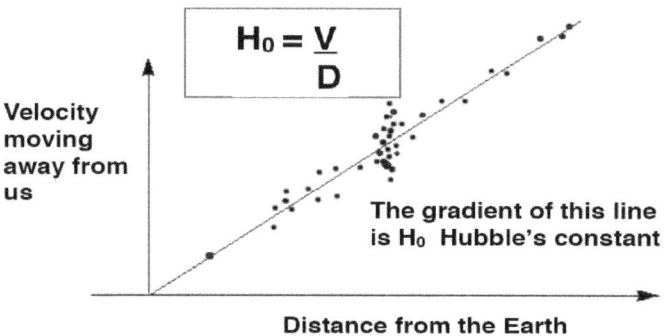

$$H_0 = \frac{V}{D}$$

Velocity moving away from us

The gradient of this line is H_0 Hubble's constant

Distance from the Earth

In other words, the farther a galaxy is from us, the faster it is moving away from us. In conclusion, the beginning of the creation of the universe with the Big Bang and the theory of expansion are proofs that the Holy Quran is from our Creator (SWT). Indeed, many scientists agree today that this big explosion could not have happened by itself without proper arrangements and prior provisions, which only Allah (SWT) have made.

> "Indeed, your Lord is Allah, who created the heavens and Earth in six days and then established Himself above the Throne. He covers the night with the day, [another night] chasing it rapidly; and [He created] the sun, the moon, and the stars, subjected by His command. Unquestionably, His is the creation and the command; blessed is Allah, Lord of the worlds"

(Quran 7:54)

Earth is the third planet from the Sun and the only astronomical object known to harbor life. Only recently have humans begun to understand the complexity of our planet. In concordance with this Quranic verse,

151

it was only a few hundred years ago that we discovered that Earth was just a tiny part of an enormous galaxy, which in turn is a small part of an even greater universe.

Astronomy in Quran

"Indeed, prayer has been decreed upon the believers a decree of specified times."

(Quran 4:103)

The Quran contains astronomical and cosmological insights across 30 chapters, reflecting Islam's integration of celestial observation with spiritual practice. Islamic religious obligations naturally fostered astronomical development: the five daily prayers occur at solar-determined times (dawn, midday, afternoon, sunset, and night), requiring precise timekeeping based on sun position. Prayer direction toward the Kaaba in Mecca necessitates geographical and astronomical calculations to determine the correct qibla from any global location. These practical religious needs transformed Muslims into skilled observers of celestial phenomena. Furthermore, the rhythms of the lunar religious calendar, most notably the fasting month of Ramadan and the two great holidays of Eid Al Fitr and Eid Al Adha, are built around observations of the moon, with each month beginning on the night that the new crescent moon is sighted.

"And it is He who ordained the stars for you that you may be guided thereby in the darkness of the land and the sea."

(Quran 6:97)

This Quranic verse tells us that the stars are there to guide humankind on land and sea. We can be anywhere in the world, and just by looking at the sky during the night, we can identify the star; we can also know what latitude we are at, where north is, and therefore all other directions. We can also know what time of the year it is in the absence of any calendar as Allah (SWT) says *"It is He who made sun a lamp and moon a light and measured stages, so you know number of years and count (of time)." ("Quran 10:5)*. The crescent moon and stars are used as signs to represent matters of religion among Muslims as Allah (SWT) says *"They ask you about new crescent moons, say they are to mark fixed times for mankind and Hajj." (Quaran 2:189)*. In this topic, the lunar calendar is one of the oldest natural calendar systems, and astronomers recognize the Islamic calendar as the only widely used lunar calendar.

This verse suggests multiple levels of cosmic organization:

'God is the One Who created seven heavens and of the earth a similar number'

(Quran 65:12).

The reference to 'seven earths' may anticipate modern exoplanet discoveries. Since 1995's first confirmed exoplanet detection, astronomers have identified thousands of worlds orbiting distant stars. Current research suggests that planetary systems represent the cosmic norm rather than rare exceptions, with potentially habitable worlds distributed throughout our galaxy, resonating with the Quranic suggestion of multiple earth-like realms.

"And We made the sky a protected ceiling, but they, from its signs, are turning away."

(Quran 21:32).

Based on this Quranic verse, the sky above the Earth is a protection for human beings. This protection is what we know today as the ozone layer (Figure). From 15 to 35 kilometers above Earth's surface, the ozone layer, or ozone shield, is a region of high ozone (O_3) concentration in the stratosphere. It is an indiscernible buffer that guards us from harmful ultraviolet (UV) radiation. In particular, the ozone layer protects us from the UV radiation, known as UV-B, which causes cancer. Long-term exposure to high levels of UV-B threatens human health and damages most animals, plants, and microbes.

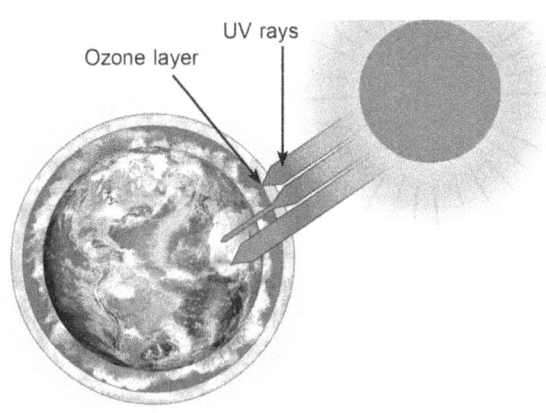

The ozone layer was discovered only in 1913 by French physicists Charles Fabry and Henri Buisson. The atmosphere around us also maintains a certain temperature suitable for our living. In the absence of this, the temperature would drop to -270°C, and we would freeze to death. The sky is also our protective covering which prevents the celestial bodies from falling on us. Allah (SWT) says in the Holy Quran *"And He restrains the sky from falling upon the Earth, unless by His permission. Indeed Allah, to the people, is Kind and Merciful" (Quran 22:65).* In conclusion, ozone layer is of the many blessings that Allah (SWT) has created it to protect the Earth so that human beings and all creatures can live on it safely.

Geology in Quran

"Allah is the One Who created seven heavens ˹in layers˺, and likewise for the Earth. The ˹divine˺ command descends between them so you may know that Allah is Most Capable of everything, and that Allah certainly encompasses all things in ˹His˺ knowledge"

(Quran 65:12).

This verse describes Earth's layered structure:

'Allah is the One Who created seven heavens in layers, and likewise for the Earth'

(Quran 65:12).

155

Modern geology identifies Earth's major layers: crust, upper mantle, transition zone, lower mantle, outer core, and inner core. Seismological studies using earthquake-generated waves revealed these internal structures, including the solid iron-nickel inner core discovered through analysis of seismic wave behavior as they traverse Earth's interior. This geological stratification demonstrates the precision of divine planetary engineering.

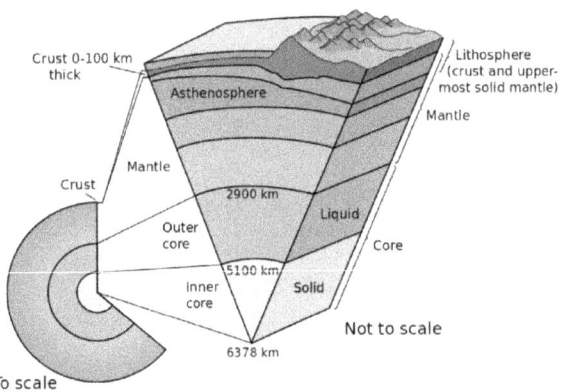

They did not discover only the dense metallic core, known as the "inner core," but it was also explained that the inner core might be different from the molten core even though both are made of the same material as the liquid core; still, this solid metal core may have other properties. They estimated that the inner metal core is about 800 miles in diameter. The size is equal to almost one percent of the volume of the Earth, which means it is much larger than other scientists previously predicted. This recent scientific discovery and the seven layers indicated in this Quranic verse proves again that the Holy Quran is the book of our Creator (SWT). On the same topic, The Prophet (SAW) also said,

"Whoever usurps even one span of land of somebody, its depth through the seven Earths will be collared to his neck "

[Saheeh Al-Bukhari, 'Book of Oppression].

These verses reveal the mountain's function:

'Have We not made the Earth a resting place? And the mountains as pegs?'

(Quran 78:6-7).

The comparison to 'pegs' suggests mountains extend deep into Earth's crust, providing stability. Modern geology confirms that mountains possess substantial underground 'roots' extending far below their visible peaks, helping stabilize continental masses and redistribute tectonic stresses. This stabilizing function was unknown in 7th-century Arabia, yet the Quranic metaphor accurately describes geological reality. It is worth noting that the description of the mountains as pegs clearly means that these mountains are not merely towering elevations that appear on the Earth's surface, but rather that their descending extensions into the Earth's lithosphere are strongly emphasized.

First, mountains develop because of the activities and impacts of massive parts (called plates) forming the Earth's crust. When the two plates collide against each other in a process called plate tectonics, the stronger one slides under the other, and the one on the top bends and forms heights and mountains.

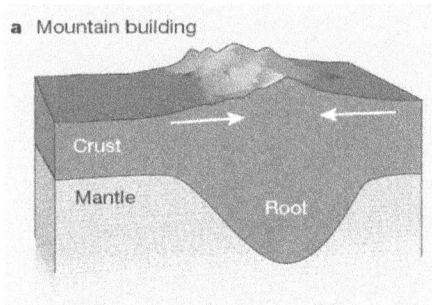

The layer beneath proceeds under the ground and makes a deep extension downward. Consequently, mountains have a portion stretching downwards, as large as their visible parts on the Earth. This is now highlighted in a book by geophysicist Frank Press called 'Earth' (1986), in which he explains how the mountains are like stakes buried deep within the Earth's surface. The author explains that mountains have underlying roots (Figure). For example, Mt. Everest, which has a height of approximately 9 km above sea level has a root deeper than 125 km.

Oceanography in Quran

This verse alludes to oceanic energy sources:

'And by the seas set on fire!'

(Quran 52:6).

Modern oceanography reveals multiple forms of 'fire' within marine environments: hydrothermal vents releasing superheated water, underwater volcanic activity, thermal energy from solar heating, and chemical energy stored in ocean currents and temperature gradients. These discoveries suggest vast renewable energy potential in oceanic systems, from thermal energy conversion to wave and current generation, validating the Quranic reference to seas containing fire-like energy.

This Quranic verse could also be an indication to use water to produce heat as by the following chemical reaction:

$$2H_2O \; \triangleright \; 2H_2 + O_2 + \text{Heat} \qquad\qquad (16)$$

This chemical reaction, known as the electrolysis of water is the decomposition of water (H_2O) into oxygen (O_2) and hydrogen gas (H_2) due to an electric current being passed through the water.

> "He released (maraja) the two seas, meeting [side by side], Between them is a barrier (barzakh) [so] neither of them transgresses."

(Quran 55:19-20)

In the same topic of seas and oceans, our blue planet contains one global ocean, five regional oceans, and seven main seas. There are numerous bodies of water around the world, and close to one hundred seas in the world that are named for the regions of the world they lie in. This Quranic verse mentions the barrier between some of them. Indeed, the Arabic word 'Barzakh' can be translated as a barrier or a partition. This barrier is not a physical partition because the Arabic word 'Maraja' literally means 'they mix with each other'.

Modern science has discovered that in the places where two different seas meet, there is a barrier between them. This barrier divides the two seas so that each sea has its own temperature, salinity, and density. However, when the water from one sea (ocean) enters the other sea (ocean), it loses its distinctive characteristics and becomes homogenized with the other sea (ocean). Oceanographers are now in a better position to explain this Quranic verse. There is a slanted, unseen water barrier between the two seas (oceans) through which water from one sea (ocean) passes to the other. In a way, this barrier serves as a transitional homogenizing area for the two waters. This phenomenon is also mentioned in the following verse of the Quran: *"And made a separating bar between the two bodies of flowing water?" (Quran 27:61).* This phenomenon occurs in several places, including the divider between the Mediterranean and the Atlantic Ocean at Gibraltar. A white bar can also be clearly seen at Cape Point, Cape Peninsula, South Africa, where the Atlantic Ocean meets the Indian Ocean.

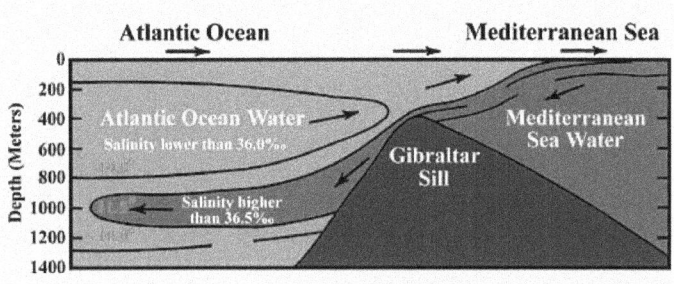

Mediterranean Sea water is warm, saline, and less dense than Atlantic Ocean water. As shown in the Figure, when Mediterranean Sea water enters the Atlantic over the Gibraltar sill, it moves several hundred kilometers into the Atlantic at a depth of about 1000 meters with its own warm, saline, and less dense characteristics. The Mediterranean water stabilizes at this depth.

> *"And it is He who has released [simultaneously] the two seas, one fresh and sweet and one salty and bitter, and He placed between them a barrier and prohibiting partition."*
>
> (Quran 25:53)

This Quranic verse is related to the separation between salty and sweet water. In this topic, modern science has discovered that in zones where fresh (sweet) and saltwater meet, the situation is somewhat different from what is found in places where two seas (oceans) meet.

When Allah (SWT) mentions the divider between fresh and salt water, it also mentions the existence of a "forbidding partition" with the barrier. The Figure shows the "forbidden partition" between the two streams. This is a recognized phenomenon which happens due to the

161

difference in densities of freshwater and seawater (denser). It has also been discovered that what distinguishes fresh water from salt water in estuaries is a **"pycnocline zone"** with a marked density discontinuity separating the two layers. This partition (zone of separation) has a different salinity from the fresh water and from the salt water.

> *"Or [they are] like darknesses within an unfathomable sea which is covered by waves, upon which are waves, over which are clouds – darknesses, some of them upon others. When one puts out his hand [therein], he can hardly see it. And he to whom Allah has not granted light – for him there is no light."*
>
> (Quran, 24:40).

Based on this Quranic verse, as the light energy travels through the water, the molecules of water scatter and absorb it. At great depths, light is so scattered that there is nothing left to detect. Related to this topic, this Quranic verse first mentions the darkness found in deep seas and oceans, where if a man stretches out his hand, he cannot see it. The darkness in deep seas and oceans is found at around a depth of 200 meters and below. At this depth, there is almost no light. Below a depth of 1000 meters, there is no light at all. Human beings are not able to dive more than forty meters without the aid of submarines or special equipment. Human beings cannot survive unaided in the deep dark part of the oceans, such as at a depth of 200 meters.

Secondly, the internal waves are also indicated in this Quranic verse (Figure). They are a type of gravity waves that circulate below the surface of the ocean, between stratified layers of water.

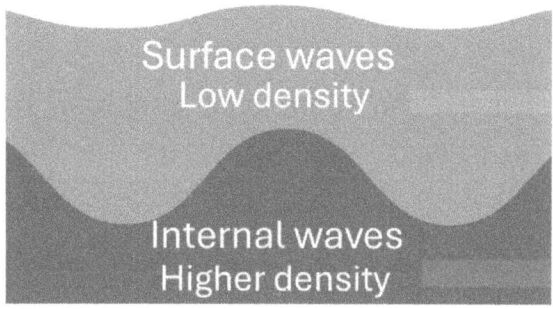

A stratified layer occurs when lower-density water is stacked above a higher-density water in the water column. Often, stratification is driven by temperature, where warmer temperature water is closer to the surface than cooler temperature water. Internal waves cannot be seen by the human eye, but they can be detected by studying temperature or salinity changes at a given location. Today's Oceanographers have stated that, unlike the belief that waves only occur on the surface, there are waves that take place internally in the oceans, below the surface of water. Invisible to the human eye, these can only be detected through special equipment. Internal waves are the source of a curious phenomenon called dead water, first reported in 1893 by the Norwegian oceanographer Fridtjof Nansen. His boat experienced strong resistance to forward motion in apparently calm conditions. To detect internal waves, Hogan et al. (2002) used the Hough transform to extract the fringes of ocean internal waves from synthetic aperture radar (SAR) images.

Muslims in Earth Sciences

In the field of geology, the approach of scientifically approximating the age of the Earth revolves around, essentially, finding the oldest piece of the planet, then figuring out how old that piece is. In this topic, Ibn Sina (980-June 1037 CE) postulated the theory of the ancient Earth in three ways. One through an examination of rocks (in line with modern geology), second through proposing that most landmass was submerged under water, and third through fossils. All three share a remarkable modern empirical style of enquiry.

Moreover, using a combination of carefully controlled observation, meticulously assembled quantitative data, and rigorous logic, Abu Rayhan Muhammad Al Biruni (973 – after 1050) deduced that there must be landmass on the other side of the globe. He concluded that somewhere in the vast expanses of ocean between Europe and Asia, there must be one or more unknown landmasses or continents. In fact, Abu Rayhan Muhammad Biruni 'scientifically' discovered America. Furthermore, free from the need to fit what he saw into a pre-existing theoretical framework, he wrote in his great work on India of what he saw "If you have seen the soil of India with your own eyes and meditate on its nature, if you consider the rounded stones found in the Earth however deeply you dig, stones that are huge near the mountains and where the rivers have a violent current and if you consider all this, you could scarcely help thinking that India has once been a sea which by degrees has been filled up by the alluvium of the streams".

Both of his insights, Land being covered with water and the processes of deposition must have taken considerable time, were the main concepts developed in the formative period of Earth Sciences in Europe by Steno, Smith, and Hutton. The results related to his scientific research was translated into Latin as early as around the 13th Century by Alfred of Sareshel, who erroneously attributed it to Aristotle. It was only in the 1660s that Nicolas Steno formulated modern concepts of deposition of horizontal strata. His work gave way to what was called the Law of superposition of strata.

> *"So whoever sights (the new moon of) the month (of Ramadan), let him fast it…"*
>
> (Quran 2:185)

In the field of astronomy and because of the importance of Islamic religious practices, Medieval Islamic astronomy comprises the astronomical developments made in the Islamic world, particularly during the Islamic Golden Age (9th–13th Centuries), and mostly written in the Arabic language. These developments mostly took place in the Middle East, Central Asia, Al-Andalus, and North Africa, and later in the Far East and India. A significant number of stars in the sky, such as Aldebaran, Altair, and Deneb, and astronomical terms such as alidade, azimuth, and nadir, are still referred to by their Arabic names. A large corpus of literature from Islamic astronomy remains today, numbering approximately 10,000 manuscripts scattered throughout the world, many of which have not been read or catalogued.

For example, Al-Aḥmad Ibn Muḥammad Ibn Kathīr Al-Farghānī (c. 800 – 870) was one of Caliph Al-Mamun's astronomers. He wrote on the astrolabe, explaining the mathematical theory behind the instrument and correcting faulty geometrical constructions of the central disc. Written in 833, his most famous book "Kitab fi Harakat Al-Samawiyah wa Jaamai Ilm al-Nujum" (Elements of Astronomy on the Celestial Motions) on cosmography contains thirty chapters including a description of the inhabited part of the Earth, its size, the distances of the heavenly bodies from the Earth and their sizes, as well as other phenomena. This textbook provided a largely non-mathematical presentation of Ptolemy's Almagest, updated with revised values from previous Islamic astronomers. The work circulated widely throughout the Islamic world and was translated into Latin during the 12th Century. It became the primary resource that European scholars used to study Ptolemaic astronomy. Other Muslim scholars who worked on astronomy receive a good treatment in The Dictionary of Scientific Biography. Amongst these astronomers:

In the same field of science, Al-Battani (d. 929) wrote The Sabian tables (Al-Zij al-Sabi), a very influential work for centuries after him. He also popularized, if not discovered, the first notions of trigonometrical ratios used today and made serious emendations to Ptolemy. His works also include the timing of the new moons, calculation of the length of the solar and sidereal year, the prediction of eclipses, and the phenomenon of parallax.

Al-Sufi (903-986) made several observations on the obliquity of the ecliptic and the motion of the sun (or the length of the solar year). He also made observations and descriptions of the stars, setting out his results constellation by constellation, discussing the stars' positions, their magnitudes, and their color, and for each constellation providing two drawings from the outside of a celestial globe, and from the inside. Finally, Al-Biruni (973-1050) claimed that the Earth rotated around its own axis. He calculated the Earth's circumference and fixed scientifically the direction of Makkah from any point of the globe. Al-Biruni wrote a total of 150 works, including 35 treatises on pure astronomy, of which only six have survived.

To conclude this third part of the book related to the Islamic contribution to natural sciences, it should mention that, after dominating the world's cultural and civilizational scene for many centuries, The Muslim Ummah slowly found itself at crisis as our cultural identities and civilizational existence were in trouble. From the beginning of the nineteenth century, the situation went from bad to worse, reaching its climax about a century later, in the first quarter of the twentieth century, when the virtually lifeless Ottoman sultanate and the weakened and largely symbolic institution of the caliphate were abolished, and many Muslim lands were divided among the major European powers.

Need for Islamization of Science

"And declare: The truth has come, and falsehood has vanished.
Indeed, falsehood is bound to vanish"

(Quran 17:81)

"Modern Western scientific methodology emerged from the Renaissance (14th-16th centuries) and Enlightenment (17th-19th centuries), emphasizing empirical observation, rational inquiry, and systematic experimentation. While these approaches yielded remarkable technological advances through two industrial revolutions, they often divorced scientific investigation from spiritual and ethical considerations. This separation created a worldview where nature exists as material to be manipulated rather than divine creation to be understood and stewarded responsibly. While the West praised and exalted knowledge at the levels of theory, validity, sources, methods (epistemology), and application, making knowledge (science) the face of Western civilization, Muslims, to a surprising degree, were underperforming in the same area. Every story of science always started in Europe or catapulted itself from Greek Antiquity to the European Renaissance. The general attitude of Western academia until recently has been of turning a blind eye to the millennia in between, which saw the flowering of a rich scientific tradition in the Muslim world.

The 20th century witnessed the widespread adoption of Western scientific education throughout the Muslim world, with institutions like Istanbul University (1900) and Cairo University (1925) serving as pioneering examples. While this educational expansion brought technological benefits, it also created intellectual tensions for Muslim students encountering materialistic assumptions embedded in secular curricula. The challenge lay not in scientific methods themselves, but in philosophical frameworks that excluded divine purpose from natural explanation. At that time, some efforts were made to harmonize science with Islam. Indeed, some Muslim scientists and scholars started to develop a spectrum of viewpoints on the place of scientific learning within the context of the Holy Quran. However, in recent years, the Muslim world's backwardness in science has been manifested by the disproportionately low amount of scientific production, measured by citations to articles published in scientific journals with an international circulation, annual expenditures on research and development, and the number of researchers and engineers. Concerns have been expressed that the contemporary Muslim world suffers from scientific illiteracy.

"Mischief has appeared on land and sea because of what the hands of men have done, that (Allah) may give them a taste of some of their deeds: in order that they may turn back (from Evil)"

(Quran 30:41).

Contemporary global challenges partly stem from viewing nature as a resource to exploit rather than a divine trust to steward. When scientific progress lacks ethical and spiritual grounding, it can lead to environmental degradation, social inequality, and technological applications that harm rather than benefit humanity. Islamic science offers an alternative paradigm that integrates empirical investigation with moral responsibility and recognition of divine purpose in creation. In fact, their pursuit of knowledge, which is primarily based on philosophy and atheism, becomes unethical and destructive when nature is treated as a material object rather than as a gift from Allah (SWT). Because of this practice, nature has undergone many changes caused by modernization and industrialization for the sole purpose of a comfortable life and economies based on consumption and profits.

As a result, the face of the Earth is constantly and rapidly deteriorating due to land, sea, and air pollution of all kinds. The main culprits behind the pollution and degradation of the quality of human life, flora and fauna are human beings themselves, as mentioned in the above Quranic verse. Moreover, the deviation from this Quranic verse: *"Indeed we have sent Our Messengers with clear proof, and revealed with them the Scripture, and the Balance that mankind may keep justice" (Quran; 57:25)* is the main source of international injustice, the increasing gap between poor and rich, the rise of poverty worldwide, global warming, the human emigration flows to rich countries, crimes, and wars.

> *"[This is] a blessed Book which We have revealed to you, that they might reflect upon its verses and that those of understanding would be reminded"*
>
> (Quran 38:29)

171

This verse calls Muslim scientists toward a comprehensive integration of revealed and empirical knowledge. The "Islamization of Science" movement seeks to develop scientific curricula that honor both rigorous empirical methods and Quranic insights, creating educational approaches where natural investigation serves spiritual development and social benefit. Rather than rejecting scientific methods, this approach transforms their underlying purpose and ethical framework. Indeed, it is widely recognized that the Holy Quran contains many hidden meanings that evolve with different interpretations as science progresses. Therefore, the correlation between the Holy Quran, the Sunnah, and recent scientific discoveries unveils further interpretations that Muslim scientists can propose for these texts.

Concluding Remarks

This exploration reveals that Allah (SWT) created the universe as humanity's ultimate classroom, where the same divine principles governing revealed guidance also operate throughout creation. The Divine Laws we have examined - Conservation of Energy, Mass, and Electrical Charge; the Law of Balance; the Laws of Charity; and the Laws of Creation and Decay - demonstrate perfect consistency between natural phenomena and Quranic teachings, affirming the unity of divine wisdom across all domains of existence. Moreover, The Divine Forces of Gravity & Magnetism are also included in the book.

This work also highlighted the remarkable convergence between Quranic descriptions of natural phenomena and modern scientific discoveries, alongside the groundbreaking contributions of Muslim scientists during Islam's Golden Age. These scholars demonstrated how Islamic principles could inspire rather than hinder scientific advancement, producing innovations that influenced global knowledge for centuries. Indeed, the Golden Age of the Islamic civilization during the period of scientific, economic, and cultural flourishing from the 8th Century to the 13th Century could be easily explained by the fact that for Muslim scholars and universities of that period used the Tawhidic paradigm as it was obligatory for them to ponder over the Holy Quran and Sunnah during these scientific research and teaching activities. On the other hand, the science of modern Western civilization is mainly based on the non-existence of the Divine Power. Consequently, based on philosophy and atheism, the Divine Forces and Divine Laws in the western scientific textbooks related to natural sciences are replaced by scientific fields related to nature such as thermodynamics and transport phenomena or given the name of scientists who discovered any aspect of these Divine Forces or Divine Laws.

Unfortunately, many universities in Muslim countries are still using these scientific textbooks copied from the Western atheistic thinking. At the same time, we have our own traditional Islamic religious schools. The challenge today for Muslim scientists is how to integrate both systems for the benefit of the Ummah. I think that it is fundamental to first" Islamize" science before the educational system. As mentioned in this book, the objective of Islamizing science is to integrate the Divine Forces and Divine Laws, Quranic verses, and the Prophet (SAW) 's sayings in the corresponding parts of scientific textbooks. Therefore, teachers should not only have the expertise in their field of science but also a good knowledge and understanding of the Noble Quran and The Prophet (SAW)'s sayings. Moreover, to revive the Islamic Golden Age, the scientific works of Muslim scientists of that period could also be added in the corresponding chapters of the textbooks.

"Islamic education ultimately aims to prepare students as Allah's vicegerents (Khalifa) on Earth, equipped with both empirical knowledge and spiritual wisdom to seek truth, serve humanity, and protect creation. This holistic approach recognizes that true education must nurture not only intellectual capabilities but also moral character, environmental consciousness, and recognition of our ultimate accountability to our Creator for how we use the knowledge He has granted us. This is the topic of my next book, Insha Allah, with a title "The Islamic Curriculum for the 21st Century".

O Allah, teach us what will benefit us, benefit us with what You have taught us, increase our knowledge, show us the truth as truth and enable us to follow it, show us falsehood as falsehood and enable us to avoid it, make us among those who listen to the word and follow the best of it, and include us by Your mercy among Your righteous servants.

lead us from the darkness of ignorance and illusion to the lights of knowledge and science, and from the mire of desires to the gardens of devotion.

Amen, O Lord of the worlds.

www.ingramcontent.com/pod-product-compliance
Lightning Source LLC
Chambersburg PA
CBHW051307120626
46547CB00015B/2130